JAMS, PICKLES AND CHUTNEYS

JAMS, PICKLES AND CHUTNEYS

David and Rose Mabey

Illustrated by M. J. Mott

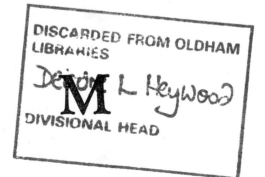

SBN 333 17682 0

First published 1975 by
MACMILLAN LONDON LTD
London and Basingstoke
Associated companies in New York
Dublin Melbourne Johannesburg and Delhi
In association with Penguin Books

Printed in Great Britain by
Western Printing Services Ltd, Bristol

for Peter and Barbara,
with thanks for Saturday suppers and Sunday lunches

'The word on the jar was RELISH . . . RELISH! What a special name for the minced pickle sweetly crushed in its white-capped jar. The man who named it, what a man he must have been. Roaring, stamping around, he must have tromped the joys of the world and jammed them in this jar and writ in a big hand, shouting RELISH!'

'Her grey eyes blinked from spectacles warped by forty years of oven-blasts and blinded by strewings of pepper and sage, so she sometimes flung corn starch over steaks, amazingly tender, succulent steaks! And sometimes dropped apricots into meat loaves, cross-pollinated meats, herbs, fruits, vegetables with no prejudice, no tolerance for recipe or formula, save that at the final moment of delivery, mouths watered, blood thundered in response.'

Dandelion Wine, Ray Bradbury, Rupert Hart-Davis, 1957

CONTENTS

ACKNOWLEDGEMENTS

While preparing this book we have been continually inspired and amazed by the cooks and housewives who developed the craft of preserving. Thanks to them much of the work has been done for us; so we are indebted to Hannah Glasse, Eliza Acton, J. Robinson Jnr. – 'a wholesale curer of comestibles' from the town of Runcorn, and many others whose names are lost.

We should also like to thank all the friends who have helped us by providing jars, recipes, fruit and vegetables from their gardens, comments and encouragements: Gordon and Elizabeth, Jenny and Alan, Rosemary and John, Mike and Pooh, Mouse and Alan, Maz, Alastair, Mrs Henman and the Onyetts. Also a special mention for 'Mum' Mabey and brother Richard, who suggested the idea and was an enthusiastic adviser.

We have received useful assistance from the Ministry of Agriculture, Fisheries and Food, the Royal Horticultural Society, Her Majesty's Stationery Office and the Campden Food Preservation Research Association and we are grateful to the staff of these organizations. Also Mrs Brown and Miss Spindler from Southwold Public Library, who dealt patiently and cheerfully with many obscure requests and overdue books.

Finally, special thanks to Miranda for the illustrations, and Jill – an understanding, tactful and friendly editor.

The publishers acknowledge with thanks the permission of the following copyright holders to reprint material: Routledge & Kegan Paul for an extract from *The Goodman of Paris* edited and translated by Eileen Power; Jonathan Cape Ltd for an extract from *Good Things in England* by Florence White; Macdonald and Co. Ltd for an extract from *Food in England* by Dorothy Hartley; National Federation of Women's Institutes for an extract from *Home-made Wines, Syrups and Cordials*.

INTRODUCTION:
SKILLS AND SECRETS

The dining-room in our house is almost completely filled by a large table. It's a tough, oaken affair with an extra section fitted by unwinding the two halves with a device rather like a crank handle; the wood creaks as it is dragged along the metal runners secured under the table and the whole mechanism is oddly reminiscent of a prototype piece of industrial revolution machinery. But our table has many uses; it has braved the weight of huge pots of curry, bottomless stews and casseroles, and has seen minute Sunday joints of breast of lamb or hand of pork carefully rationed to last two of us for a hot meal and a cold supper. It is, above all, a meeting place.

This vast wooden slab is also a perfect working surface. By now it is seasoned with the sting of onions and vinegar, the vapours of oranges and lemons, and there is enough space for peeling and chopping, grating, squeezing and slicing. But it's appropriate that it should be so, since the other main feature of our dining-room is the preserve cupboard. Here the produce is stored. Conditions inside the cupboard are ideal – it is dark, cool and dry, and conveniently placed so that a jar can be taken out while we are at the table eating.

But why do we bother with these preserves when it is so easy to visit the supermarket or grocer's shop with its rows of inviting jams and chutneys, ketchups and pickles? There are reasons, and good ones too. They have to do with economics, with the quality of home-made preserves, and with the craft of preserving. Actually the word 'preserving' itself seems to be in conflict with many current attitudes to cookery; there are implications of 'saving' and utilizing excess food, a feeling of permanence when the fashion is for temporary and 'instant' foods. It's a paradox that the most sophisticated techniques of the food scientists aren't primarily geared to providing us with new tastes and *better* food, but to the reduction of food to its basic level – that of fuel. Of course it would be hard to deny that technology has radically altered our eating habits, or that it has raised the general level of nourishment. And convenience food *does* have its uses. But we must learn to use it properly, when it is necessary, and not allow it to completely dominate our attitudes to cookery.

Home-made jams and pickles may seem out of place in such a world, but the skills of preserving can have a significant effect on our eating habits, arguably even more so these days when the wastage and misuse of food is so prominent; so the notion of saving and utilizing excess fruit and vegetables, at least in individual households, *is* important.

The business of preserving really begins outside the kitchen, either with seed planting or a summer excursion along hedgerows; it may even start with a tour of greengrocers' shops, a hunt for bargain fruit and vegetables. After planting, growth and harvesting are complete, then the preserve belongs in the kitchen and on the table. There tends to be too much emphasis on the fact that preserves are quick and easy to make. This misses the point. It is true that most of the recipes are quite straightforward, yet the whole process demands a leisurely approach and above all patience. So don't be tempted to hurry or rush through the actual preparations. You will need time to get the ingredients ready, and you will need to watch as the preserve cooks, stirring, testing and adjusting the flavour and consistency until you are satisfied. And when the preserve is bottled and stored away, you will have to wait for weeks or even months before it can be put on the table and opened.

More than anything, preserving is fun, and although it involves laborious preparation and weeks of patient waiting, the product always seems to justify the work. It is partly the realization that those shallots planted on a dreary February afternoon have provided a winter's supply of pickled onions; also the sheer enjoyment of unexpected flavours, the combinations of fruit and vegetables, and the sight of friends enjoying what you have made.

Ultimately the best preserves derive from a tricky blend of intuition, imagination and understanding. This is at the heart of preserving; it should dictate the way we make preserves and also how we use them. In this book Rose and I have attempted to show how we solve some of these problems. It is, intentionally, a very personal view of the subject, a record of what *we* do, what can go wrong and how *we* put it right. There are difficulties and drawbacks, but preserving is also full of unexpected discoveries and simple joys. In a small way it provides a thread of continuity, a sense of balance so that the growing of food, its preservation and its uses can be seen as part of one process, inevitably controlled by the seasons, but developed out of individual resourcefulness and imagination.

David Mabey
Wenhaston, 1974

Chapter 1

ESSENTIALS

The Theory of Preservation

The main object of preservation has always been to keep or 'save' food in a good condition for long periods of time. This derived from the need to provide winter supplies from crops that were only available during the summer months, and to prevent wastage when there was a glut of fruit or vegetables. Numerous methods and techniques were devised to ensure that food did not decay, but later another aspect of preservation emerged; techniques that had originally been used out of necessity were adapted because the products themselves were interesting to eat.

5

There are two causes of deterioration in food. Firstly the action of enzymes in the foods themselves; these are responsible for the natural breakdown of the food and cause among other things the browning of cut surfaces and the change from pectin to pectic acid that occurs in over-ripe fruit. Secondly the growth of all forms of micro-organisms, for instance yeasts, moulds and bacteria. Most traditional forms of preservation are aimed at preventing the access and growth of these micro-organisms.

Drying is one of the oldest methods of food preservation, but not until quite recently was the reason for its effectiveness known. Originally our ancestors dried fruit and vegetables simply because they knew that this would prevent their supplies going bad, but they did not know why this was. In fact, micro-organisms need moisture to grow. If food is dried and moisture removed, then the growth of bacteria and yeasts is prevented; the food does not decompose and enzyme activity is stopped. Of course once foods have been dried, they should be stored in such a way that moisture is not re-absorbed.

Another important method involves the use of chemical preservatives, of which the most commonly used are salt, sugar, vinegar and alcohol. Salt, either dry or in the form of brine, will prevent the growth of micro-organisms without affecting the value of the food as such. The same applies to sugar; yeasts and moulds are particularly active in fermenting sugars, but are unable to grow in high concentrations such as those used in jams. However most yeasts and moulds are harmless to man, and if any growth does occur on the surface of jam, the mould and the jam immediately below it should simply be spooned off and thrown away. The rest is quite safe to use. Vinegar and alcohol (usually in the form of spirits such as brandy) are both good preservatives and prevent the growth of micro-organisms.

There are other methods that do not involve the use of any preservative, but depend on the fact that micro-organisms are affected by extremes of temperatures. This is the principle behind bottling, canning and freezing. In bottling and canning, these organisms are destroyed by heat and enzyme activity is stopped. Deep freezing has a similar effect. Accuracy of temperature control and the right conditions are vitally important to the success of all these methods.

Fruit and Vegetables

There are three main sources for the fruit and vegetables used in preserving. First the garden. Most produce is not grown specifically to make preserves (shallots are a notable exception), but where possible a quantity of the crop should be preserved. We have not dwelt on the growth and cultivation of fruit and vegetables in the garden except where it relates specifically to preservation. There are any number of good publications available that will give all the information needed. Two very useful little books are *The Kitchen Garden* by Brian Furner (Pan), and *The Small Garden* by C. E. Lucas Phillips (Pan).

Secondly produce can be got from markets and greengrocers' shops. In the recipes we have indicated what characteristics are necessary for particular preserves – age, colour, shape, variety. The important thing is to look for bargains and buy in bulk when you find them.

The third source is wild food. Berries, nuts and fungi are particularly valuable here, but the range of foods and their uses is enormous. We have described quite a number in the book, but readers should consult a guide if they are unsure about identification (*particularly with fungi*), and the whole subject is covered in *Food for Free* by Richard Mabey (Collins). Readers should also consult guides such as *The Oxford Book of Food Plants* where necessary.

Equipment

From your standard kitchenware you will need sharp steel knives, a large wooden chopping board, a colander, scales (preferably with a large pan), a plastic funnel, a stainless steel sieve, various mixing bowls and saucepans. In addition there are one or two items required specially for preserving.

Wooden spoons: these are very important and a set should be kept for preserving. Do not use metal spoons when dealing with vinegar.

Earthenware crock: this is a useful item for salting beans and for making pickles that require a large container, e.g. marrow mangoes.

Preserving pan: the essential piece of equipment for making jams, jellies, marmalades, chutneys and ketchups. It should be large, made of aluminium with handles that make lifting a pan full of hot preserve relatively easy and safe.

Jelly bag: this conical fabric strainer is the best way to strain a jelly. Improvised methods such as old stockings can be used but the jelly bag is the most practical and successful. You can buy stands for use with jelly bags, but more usually an upturned chair serves quite well; the bag is tied between the legs of the chair.

Jam thermometer: when making jam, a special thermometer may be useful for determining setting point. Keep it in a safe place. Before you use it to test jam, put it into hot water and return it to the water after using.

Containers: you will need a good selection of jars and pots for preserving, so collect empty jam jars, instant coffee jars, ketchup bottles etc., from friends. It is surprising what can be useful – a friend of ours salvages empty tonic-water bottles (the non-returnable sort) and uses them for her tomato ketchup. Large jars, such as might be needed for pickling onions, can sometimes be got from hotels and restaurants when they have finished with their catering-size bottles of mayonnaise or pickled gherkins. Jars should be thoroughly cleaned before use and dried in a warm oven or under the grill so that they do not crack on meeting hot jam or chutney; but don't let the jars get hot, or the jam will boil in them.

Covers: a great variety of covers can be used, and we have outlined the best ways for each type of preserve. The most useful covers are those that can be bought from stationers and other shops in packets. These contain waxed discs, cellophane covers, rubber bands and labels, and are very handy for most types of preserve except pickles. Place the waxed disc on the surface of the preserve directly after potting, wax side down, so that it lies flat and no airspace is left. Then wipe one side of the cellophane cover with a damp cloth, put this over the jar, damp side up, and fix with a rubber band. Finally label the jar with its name and the date it was made.

A Note about the Recipes

The recipes in this book are confined to the type of preserve made and used in the British Isles, America and to some extent in Europe; in oriental cookery, preserves belong to a different tradition, based on different principles and applications. This is a personal selection too;

there are many more preserves that could be included, but we have chosen ones that we know and like and which are representative of the various types.

We have had to adapt many of the recipes we have found or been given, and this process of alteration, varying ingredients and techniques is part of the business of preparing a cookery book. But the same flexibility should be passed on to the reader; so what we have given are guidelines, recipes that work for us and suit our tastes. You should adapt them when you feel it necessary, experiment with new combinations and invent imaginative uses for these preserves.

PART ONE

Chapter 2

STORAGE

Storage is really the simplest method of preserving, and the most practical products to store are root vegetables, nuts, some hard fruit and eggs. Green vegetables and soft fruit don't store well and are best preserved by other methods.

It is interesting to compare, for instance, eggs stored in isinglass and eggs preserved by pickling, as the products are very different. Pickling brings about a transformation – a change in the whole character of the egg, its taste and texture and even what it looks like. Many of the oldest methods of preserving such as drying and salting have a great deal in common with the notion of storage – simply saving food supplies in a palatable condition. Pickles, jams and chutneys altered this notion so that it became more than a task performed out of necessity; these products had special qualities as foods, and this is now primarily why we make them. But we should keep in mind the more functional aspects of preserving.

There are various techniques for storing fruit and vegetables and it is useful to look at these and compare them with other, more elaborate methods of preservation.

Vegetables

Root vegetables (carrots, beetroot, potatoes, turnips and swedes): after lifting, the vegetables should be cleaned by removing any excess earth and dirt carefully. Before actually storing it is best to allow the roots to dry off for a short while. The green tops should be twisted off. Carrots are best put layer by layer into boxes with sand; wood ash is recommended for beetroot. Potatoes and swedes can be stored in nets. The vegetables should be kept in a cool outhouse or cellar and protected from frost and mice. Potatoes must also be protected from the light, to prevent them turning green.

Onions: these should be lifted when the leaves are yellow and drooping, and laid out to dry either in the sun or in a warm dry place indoors. The leaves can then be twisted off and the onions stored in nets, or plaited into strings and hung up. The important thing is that they should be well ventilated otherwise they will tend to sprout.

Marrows, melons and pumpkins: these should be cut before the first frosts and stored in nets.

Other vegetables, notably parsnips, leeks, celery and Jerusalem artichokes, are best left in the ground and dug up as required. The fact that they keep well like this is one of the reasons why they hardly ever figure in preserving. Of course this is very convenient, and the vegetables themselves are actually improved by being left in the ground, for example frosts help to increase the sugar content and thus the flavour of parsnips.

Fruit

Apples and pears: these can be usefully stored for several months, but only completely sound fruit must be used; bruises, scars or blemishes are ideal sites for micro-organisms, and you will learn to your cost the dangers of 'the rotten apple'. These less-than-perfect fruit together with windfalls are best preserved by other methods.

It is a general rule that early varieties of apples and pears do not keep well, and should be eaten up fresh. Store only the late varieties and don't pick them before they are fully matured. After picking, the fruit should be left to stand in a cool place overnight.

The best places for storing are cellars or outbuildings protected from the weather. They should be cool, dark and moist and preferably with a fairly constant temperature. The fruit can be stored in trays in single layers. You can buy moulded trays quite cheaply which are very useful since their design allows a free flow of air around the fruit.

Another method that is very successful with small quantities of fruit is to tie them in old stockings, knotting the stocking between each fruit so that there is no contact between them. These filled stockings can be hung up in cellars or outbuildings.

Oranges and lemons: these keep quite well and are normally stored in nets. One old way of storing lemons involved passing a strong thread through the 'nib end' of the fruit and hanging up the strings from the ceiling of a dry airy room.

Nuts

Most nuts can be stored and kept through the winter, which is useful since drying and other methods of preserving are often inadvisable.

Walnuts: collect them when they fall to the ground, remove the husks and scrub the shells free of any fibrous material. Dry the nuts at room temperature. Store them in a large jar or earthenware crock by alternating a layer of nuts with a layer of equal quantities of salt and coconut fibre (or sawdust, bulb fibre or dry hardwood shavings). Mrs Beeton suggests that a layer of damp hay be put on top of the nuts before covering the crock. After packing, the nuts should be kept in a cool place.

Hazelnuts: gather them in September or October when the husks have dried out and put them in single layers on trays in a cool, airy room. Turn them occasionally.

Eggs

There were a great number of methods for 'preserving eggs fresh' for weeks or months. Often they were first scalded in boiling water, then packed in bran or sawdust. For sea voyages they were sometimes covered with salted butter or oil before packing. Another method was to keep them in a solution of lime water in a cellar. Eliza Acton gives a delicate method that involves varnishing the eggs with gum arabic; this operation should be done in stages. Half the egg should be coated and allowed to dry before the remainder is applied. This prevents any of the wet gum being rubbed off during handling.

This technique would seem to be the predecessor of the method used today which involves immersing the eggs in isinglass. This is sometimes known as 'water glass', and can be bought as a powder at the chemist's. Mix it as directed and immerse as many clean new-laid eggs as the water glass will contain. A large pail may be useful for this.

There is also a patent liquid paraffin wax called 'Oteg' that can be used. The eggs are dipped in this and then stored in cartons in a cool cupboard or larder until required.

Chapter 3

DRYING

It is clear from archaeological evidence that the preservation of fruit and vegetables by drying has a very long history indeed. Prehistoric Swiss lake dwellings have revealed, among other things, remains of small sour crabapples and also large apples which may well have been cultivated; these are often cut in two which seems to suggest that they were dried. The process of drying probably originated as a way of imitating effects seen in nature – the action of sun and wind on fruit and vegetables. Our ancestors had no notion of the reasons why drying worked, only that it seemed to preserve their summer fruits throughout the winter. No doubt the process became linked to myth and superstition since sun and air were both agencies with strong magical associations.

Dried fruit was very important to many of the ancient civilizations, particularly in Egypt and Mesopotamia. Figs, dates and grapes were all dried, either in the sun or by burying them in hot sand. They were essential items of trade and were also used extensively in cookery either in dishes with meat and fish, or as sweetmeats.

But it was in Rome that dried fruits really developed as items of cookery. Dried apples, onions and pears were essential to country people as winter food, and Roman cooks developed outlandish uses for dried fruits of all kinds to satisfy the gluttonous demands of the ruling classes. They even transformed the process of drying itself into an elaborate feat of cookery; Apicius suggests that figs should first be squashed by treading, then mixed with toasted sesame seed, anise, fennel seed and cummin. This mixture was made into balls and wrapped appropriately in fig leaves, which were dried and stored in jars.

Dried fruit continued to be used extensively in the Middle East after the fall of the Roman Empire, and much of the character of high medieval cookery is derived from the Arab kitchen. Combinations of dried fruit with meat, fish and even vegetables were common to both; for example a typical medieval fish pie would consist of pickled herrings, raisins, dates and cinnamon, all encased in a 'coffin' of pastry and baked. Medieval cooks also made use of prunes (dried plums) and 'raisins of Corinth'. These were the small dried grapes that are now known as 'currants'; the name is simply a corruption of Corinth, and is nothing to do with blackcurrants.

Dried vegetables were also used extensively, particularly by poorer people. Peas and beans were dried and either made into a kind of porridge – the ancestor of our own pease pudding – or mixed with salt bacon. Peasant wives also made 'bean butter', dried beans cooked to a mush in mutton broth and spread on oatcakes or coarse bread.

All these items, both fruit and vegetables, were very important when the sea trade routes to the Indies were opened up in the seventeenth century, and there was a need for food supplies that would stand up to the conditions and time scale of long voyages. Records indicate that 'shipboard persons of credit' took with them dried pears, prunes, barrelled figs and 'raisins of the sunne'.

The methods of sun drying used in the Mediterranean and Middle East for figs, dates and grapes were tricky and hardly successful in a more northerly climate, so alternative methods were devised. Vegetables like peas and beans were simply air dried, while fruit was often saturated with sugar and then dried. This technique was developed in the eighteenth century and a great many recipes for treating apricots, gooseberries, plums, quinces and peaches have been handed down to us. No doubt this was an attempt to emulate the texture and taste of exotic dried fruits like dates, which were sweet, sticky and chewy.

In 1780 the first patent for drying vegetables was issued. This involved scalding green vegetables and then allowing them to dry in a heated room. Later numerous ingenious methods of drying were devised; for instance, the method patented by Edwards in 1840 for drying potatoes involved boiling them until the skins cracked, and pressing them through small holes in perforated cylinders. The threads of pulp were dried on steam-heated tables.

The latter part of the nineteenth century brought the first attempts to dry vegetables at a low temperature, the forerunner of many of today's freeze drying processes, and dessicated soups were developed at the same time as that symbol of wartime austerity – dried egg.

Today the freezing of fresh fruit and vegetables has superseded many of the older methods of preserving, but there is still an important market for packet soups, dried pulses, instant mashed potato and many others. Raisins and other dried fruit are in great demand, and nowadays each fruit is coated in a film of liquid paraffin. This is probably harmless enough; the paraffin prevents moisture attacking the fruit since packets are often stored carelessly after opening. The paraffin coating might also prevent the fruit from coalescing into a huge, sticky lump.

General

1. In countries where the climate is hot, sun drying is still used, especially for fruit. But unless the process is carefully watched there is a danger that the flesh at the centre of the fruit may not be completely desiccated; this leads to the growth of bacteria, and the fruit spoils. Conditions in this country are much better suited to air drying with artificial heat. The requirements for drying are good ventilation and

movement of air together with the correct temperature maintained for a sufficient length of time. Any kitchen oven will satisfy these demands.

We have normally given drying temperatures in degrees Fahrenheit. These temperatures tend to be below the gas regulo scale so readers who use gas ovens should simply turn the gas as low as possible, leave the oven door ajar and be careful to ensure that the small gas jet is not extinguished by draughts.

Solid fuel stoves such as the Aga can also be used for drying. Here again there may be difficulties, but those familiar with these stoves should be able to maintain a suitably low temperature. It is best to use the lower 'simmering oven' for drying, and to leave the door ajar.

2. When the produce has been prepared it should be put in the oven on trays which allow free circulation of air. A shallow baking tin can be used provided the produce is turned frequently during drying. In all cases it is important that it is arranged in a single layer making sure that each piece is separate and does not touch or obscure its neighbour.

3. The oven temperature should be slowly raised to about 120–150°F depending on the produce. If it is dried too quickly the outside hardens and this can have bad effects on the final product; it may prevent the loss of moisture from the centre or in the case of plums cause split skins. The oven door should be left ajar to give a free movement of air. The drying can be done in one stage, or in several shorter stages over 2 or 3 days. The time needed to dry various kinds of produce varies. For example, apple rings normally take about 5 hours; small mushrooms dry in a shorter time, while fat, fleshy plums take a good deal longer to dry completely. So you will need to organize a drying session in advance, particularly if you intend to do it in stages. In this case you should keep the produce covered in a dry place between each stage.

4. You can test when the produce is ready by squeezing a piece between the fingers. If there is no sign of moisture the fruit is completely dried. It should then be removed from the oven and allowed to stand at room temperature in a dry place for 12 hours.

5. If dried fruit and vegetables are soaked correctly before use, they will take approximately the same time to cook as their fresh equivalents.

Fruit

1. Ripe fruit should be used. It dries quickly, keeps well and has a good flavour. Drying is most successful with firm fruit such as apples and pears, apricots, plums and gooseberries.

2. Dried fruit should be packed in single layers in wooden or cardboard boxes lined with greaseproof paper. These should be stored in a dry place.

3. When dried fruit is used it is important to give it a long soaking (24–48 hours depending on the fruit) in plenty of water before cooking. If sugar is to be added, this should be done a few minutes before the fruit is completely cooked.

Vegetables

1. Use young fresh vegetables. Peas, mushrooms and beans of various types are best for drying.

2. When they have been prepared vegetables should be scalded in boiling water for 2 to 5 minutes, then drained and dried. There are some exceptions, such as mushrooms.

3. Dried vegetables should be stored in tightly corked bottles and protected from the light.

4. They need to be soaked in water before being used, but only for 12 hours at the most. They are then cooked in salted water until tender.

Dried Mushrooms

There are a number of different ways of drying mushrooms, but they are all quite simple, and need no special equipment. The only requirements are a warm, dry atmosphere and good ventilation. The best mushrooms to use for drying are field mushrooms (*Agaricus campestris*) that have opened flat and are beginning to go dark underneath. Fairy ring 'champignons' (*Marasmius oreades*) are also very good. In all cases the stalks should be removed before drying.

Oven-dried: remove the stalks from the mushrooms, and wipe the flaps with a slightly damp cloth. Place them on a flat baking sheet or arrange them on the shelves of a cool oven (not more than 120°F), so

22

that they do not touch one another. Leave them with the door ajar to allow good ventilation, until they are absolutely dry and feel crisp to the touch. They can then be stored in airtight containers until required. If you wish you can make a powder by simply crumbling the dried mushrooms.

Another method of oven drying is to thread the mushrooms onto thin sticks of wood making sure there is airspace between each mushroom. These twigs can be put in rows like a grid across the oven ledges. It is a good idea to put the mushrooms into the oven after it has been used and is cooling off; this may mean that the process of drying takes several days (or nights) but it does save on fuel.

Air-dried: the prepared mushrooms can be threaded onto a length of string using a darning needle, and either hung from the ceiling in a warm dry room or in an airing cupboard until they are dry and crisp. It is sensible to knot the string between each mushroom to prevent any contact during drying.

A rather fanciful, but nevertheless quite practical method is to get a twiggy hawthorn bough, and impale the mushrooms onto the thorns. Plant the 'mushroom tree' in a flower pot or other container so that it is wedged upright, and leave it before the fire, turning the whole thing round occasionally. This method is particularly useful for small mushrooms when an oven is not available.

Dried mushrooms can be easily re-constituted when required by soaking in tepid water. They can be used to make soups, thrown dry into stews and casseroles, or chopped into omelettes. In the gloomy, sparse months of late winter such treats are greatly treasured. They can transform routine meals and revive flagging spirits.

Dried French and Runner Beans
You must use only the youngest and most tender beans. Top and tail them and string if necessary; cut them into pieces about 2 inches long and then blanch them in boiling water for a couple of minutes. Make sure you drain them thoroughly, and then lay them out on trays to dry. They should be spread out in a single layer so that the pieces do not touch or obscure one another. The easiest way to dry them is in a cooling

oven with the door ajar. During the drying process you may need to turn the beans to ensure that they are fully exposed to the air.

You can test whether the beans are completely dried or not by breaking a piece between your fingers; if it is crisp and brittle then it is ready, and the beans can be packed into jars, well covered and stored in a dry, dark cupboard.

Dried Peas

It is essential to use the very young pods. The peas can be left to dry as whole pods on the plant, then shelled and stored in a dry place; this is the method used commercially for drying marrowfat peas. More usually however the peas are picked and dried *after* shelling. (The pods should not be thrown away but should be kept and used to make soup or pea-pod wine.) The method of drying suggested by Hannah Glasse in the eighteenth century needs slight adaptation as regards packing and storage, but is essentially quite satisfactory:

Take fine young peas, shell them, throw them into boiling water with some salt in, let them boil five or six minutes, throw them into a cullender to drain; then lay a cloth four or five times double on a table, and spread them on; dry them very well; and have your bottles ready, fill them and cover them with mutton-fat tried; when it is a little cool, fill the necks almost to the top, cork them, tie a bladder and a lath over them, and set them in a cool dry place.

The Art of Cookery Made Plain and Easy, Hannah Glasse, 1747

When the peas are required for use let them soak overnight. Then they can be cooked and served without fear that they will be hard or cooked for so long that they begin to disintegrate.

Dried Horseradish

Horseradish is easy to find, its huge green leaves are unmistakable on wasteground and railway embankments. It is a perennial and its complex root system can only be got at successfully with a spade. Dig up sufficient horseradish for your use – you won't be able to get out the complete root unless you are prepared to dig a fairly large patch of ground, but pieces can be chopped off with the spade. When you have secured enough, go home and wash and scrape the pieces.

Rose had warned me about the overpowering fumes of freshly grated horseradish, but I foolishly expected little more than the effects from strong onions. My first scraping session proved me agonisingly wrong. Having washed the horseradish and peeled it, I noticed a faintly suspicious smell, but this was nothing compared to the choking fumes that poured from the grated roots. I had opened all doors and windows in the kitchen, but to little effect; the fumes assaulted my eyes, nose and throat. I was convinced that I should never get the stuff grated, or if I did I would be near asphyxiation. But eventually it was done and I staggered out into the fresh air.

Once the horseradish has been grated it should be spread out on a flat tin and dried at the bottom of a cool oven. It should be turned and moved around so that it dries completely. When this is done pack it into warm, *dry* jars with an airtight seal.

Although the freshly grated root has the best flavour and highest potency, it does dry quite successfully, but make sure that the container is *completely* airtight. Dried horseradish is particularly useful for making up horseradish sauce, and it can be used in place of the fresh root in marrow mangoes and store sauces.

Dried Apples

Traditionally apples were dried by coring with a bone corer and then threading them whole on strings suspended from the ceiling. Nowadays they are usually dried in rings and this is a good way of making use of excess windfalls.

First peel and core the apples carefully making sure that you do not damage the fruit in the process. Cut the apples into rings about $\frac{1}{4}$ inch thick and immediately put these into a pan of salt water ($\frac{1}{4}$ oz. salt per pint). This helps to prevent the fruit browning during preparation. After a few minutes remove the rings, dry off any excess water and arrange them in single layers on trays, ensuring that individual pieces do not touch or obscure one another. Put the trays into a cool oven (not more than 140°F) with the door ajar to allow a free flow of air. The drying can be done economically by putting the trays in when the oven is cooling down after it has been used for baking. The process can be completed in one stage, in which case the rings will be dry after about 4–6 hours. If a cooling oven is used, the process can be divided into several stages without any problem. When the rings are drying they can be turned although this isn't essential so long as they are given sufficient time in the oven. The best way of telling if they are ready is by texture; they should have a texture resembling chamois leather, with its dry spongy feel. At this stage they should be removed from the oven and allowed to stand at room temperature in a dry place for about 12 hours. Ideally they should be packed in wooden boxes, in layers separated by greaseproof paper, and stored in a dry place.

Dried apple rings have many uses. They can provide apple sauce for roast pork, when there are no fresh apples in the house, or they can be chopped and used with other dried fruit in cake mixtures. While much dried fruit needs a long soaking before it is used, apples can be reconstituted quite easily by stewing in water for 2–3 hours. If sugar, lemon peel and a few cloves are added near the end of the cooking, this makes a delicious and simple dessert.

Norfolk Biffins: these were very hard apples with a sweet taste and firm red skins. Parson Woodforde, the eighteenth-century diarist who spent much of his later life as curate of Weston Longville in Norfolk, was very proud of his special 'beefan' apple tree. On 3 October 1800 he picked a monster apple weighing 13 ounces, which won him a wager of sixpence.

Biffins were dried whole in old brick ovens and then flattened and dried further. This process was repeated until a cake about 1 inch thick was obtained. The special point about these dried biffins was that the fruit was dried whole and the flesh inside was partially converted to juice; if the skin burst the apples were ruined. Eliza Acton thought that these were in many ways superior to the apples offered for sale fresh in her time. Sadly they seem to have declined since then.

Dried Pears

Pears can be dried like apples, peeled, cored and cut into quarters or eighths. They should be kept in salt water before drying, then the method used for apples can be followed.

Another method common in the seventeenth and eighteenth centuries involved boiling pears in a mixture of equal parts thin honey, water and 'small beer' (good draught bitter would be a useful substitute today). When the pears were tender they were allowed to drain on a rack and then dried in a warm oven.

Dried Plums (Prunes)

The best plums for making prunes are the dark-skinned, fleshy varieties such as 'Prune d'Agen', 'Prince Engelbert', and 'Fellemberg'. First wipe the fruit with a damp cloth and lay it on trays. Then dry in the oven. The temperature of the oven should be low to begin with, and increased slowly to ensure that the plum skins do not split. Raise the temperature of the oven slowly to 120°F and leave the plums until the skins begin to shrivel; you can then increase the temperature to 150°F and allow the plums to dry completely.

The fruit is sufficiently dried if it yields no juice when squeezed between the fingers. The prunes can then be removed, allowed to stand at room temperature in a dry place for 12 hours, and then packed and stored.

When you wish to make use of the prunes, remember that they need to be well soaked first; there are various methods of doing this – you can use water, cold tea or brandy depending on the circumstances. And remember too the old ways of using prunes. They should be part of succulent dishes like matelote of eel, eaten with rabbit or hare, or used as a stuffing for turkey, and they make small masterpieces with smoked haddock and with bacon.

Dried Apricots

Choose apricots that are fresh, sound and just ripe. First wipe with a damp cloth, split and remove the stones. Weigh the total amount of fruit left, and put it into a dish. Then strew with sugar (12 oz. for every pound of fruit) and leave overnight. Next day transfer the apricots to a preserving pan and simmer gently until they are just tender. This should take 5–10 minutes. Put the fruit and syrup into a pan, cover it and leave for 2 days. Then remove the apricots carefully, allow them to drain and put them onto trays in single layers so that the pieces do not touch one another. Leave them in a cool oven (about 120°F) until they have dried. Test them by squeezing a fruit between your fingers; if no moisture exudes it is sufficiently dried and the fruit can be packed and stored in a dry place until required.

When the apricots are to be used it is important to soak them in water for a sufficient length of time before cooking, otherwise the fruit will not be tender or juicy. At least 12 hours should be allowed for soaking, in fact the longer the better. Then they should be brought to the boil slowly and cooked until the fruit is soft. If more sugar needs to be added it should be put in near the end of the cooking time.

Dried apricots have a great number of uses; they make excellent jam and chutney; they can be added to marmalade; chopped and used in cake mixtures; stewed and served with other fruit as a dessert with fresh cream.

They are also an essential ingredient in many Persian dishes, especially combined with lamb. There is a traditional lamb and apricot stew called 'mishmishiya', a name derived from the Arabic word 'mishmish' meaning apricot, which has been adapted to form the basis of a lamb and apricot pilaff or 'polo'. Dried apricots are also used, together with prunes and raisins as a stuffing for roast chicken. Fruit can also be combined with vegetables, and there is a marvellous dish that blends dried apricots with stuffed courgettes. (Readers should consult *A Book of Middle Eastern Food* by Claudia Roden (Penguin) for more information and detailed recipes.)

The method of drying used for apricots is also applicable to gooseberries (which are first cut open and de-seeded), and other firm fruit. It was originally a method of producing a type of chewy sweetmeat, rather than simply a way of storing fruit. (Compare with Candied Fruit and Flowers, pp. 165–9.)

Dried Herbs

Herbs spread unchecked in our garden. There's no imposed discipline, no organization or separation into distinct species; we allow the plants to grow where they will. When a herb is thriving it matters little if it occupies an allotted piece of ground or seeds itself on the edge of a concrete path. And the eradication of plants because they do not comply with one's plans of an organized garden is senseless.

Before we arrived there was a semblance of order. An area in one corner of the vegetable patch was given over to herbs. The centrepiece was a thriving bay tree with clumps of downy applemint and spearmint completely surrounding it. There was parsley as well, but already this had strayed onto the paths and into the rose-beds. We moved into the house in late autumn, and it wasn't until early spring that we noticed the bright green stems of chives among the twitch-grass that we were clearing from the vegetable patch. We later found a diminutive sage plant almost submerged beneath mint and parsley, and then lemon balm. Across the garden, on the far side of the vegetable patch, bushes of rosemary and wormwood were growing beneath white lilacs.

In the winter months when it is no longer possible to go out into the garden to pick sprigs of fresh mint or bundles of chives, dried herbs

have an important place in the kitchen. This is why bunches are gathered in the summer and dried; it is a way of ensuring a supply of flavours for the soups, stews and casseroles of winter. Whether you are picking fresh herbs from your garden or from the wild, the best time to gather them is just before the plants come into flower. The aromatic oils which give each herb its characteristic smell and flavour are at this time still mainly concentrated in the leaves. Ideally you should choose a dry sunny morning for gathering; if picked wet, the herbs are likely to decay, and if exposed to strong afternoon sunshine they will tend to lose some of their volatile oils. Simply pick the stalks intact and remove any shrivelled or blemished leaves. It is also worth drying the seeds of herbs such as dill. Gather the seed heads when they are ripe on a dry day and treat them like leafy herb-stalks.

The best way of actually drying the herbs is also the simplest. Tie the stalks in bundles and hang them to dry in a warm, dry well-ventilated room. The kitchen can be as good a place as any, although unless it is well ventilated, the steam issuing from pans of boiling vegetables can ruin the drying stalks. A large airing cupboard is possibly the ideal site if you do not object to sheets and blankets that are scented with mint or fennel. The drying process takes about two weeks, during which time the bundles should be turned around several times to ensure that all the leaves are fully exposed to the warm air. You can tell when the herbs are ready by simply crumbling a leaf between your fingers; if it is crisp and breaks up easily then it is dry. Next strip the leaves and any dried flower heads from the stalks and crumble them onto a sheet of clean paper. Pack the dried herbs into clean, dry jars with an airtight seal, label them and store in a dry cupboard.

When you come to use dried herbs remember that, because of dehydration, they are much more concentrated than their fresh counterparts. Dried herbs are roughly three times as strong as fresh herbs.

Suggestions for the most useful herbs to dry (those in brackets are the least successful, but are worth attempting):

(Lemon balm)	(Parsley)
Sweet basil	Rosemary
Bay leaves	Sage
Chervil	Savory
(Chives)	(French tarragon)
Fennel	Thyme – various varieties
Marjoram	Mint – various varieties

Of course drying is most sensibly used for those herbs that lie dormant over the winter months like chives and mint. But even those such as thyme which are available fresh throughout the year ought to be dried in case of emergencies.

Bear in mind that dried herbs do not keep their flavour and scent indefinitely; they should be used up within 6 months of drying, although you may find that they will last until the next season's fresh herbs are ready to be dried. If you have the space, it is best to use dried herbs straight from the stalk, rather than from the jar. Herb stalks and twigs can be used in stocks and for flavouring roast meat.

It is interesting that herbs grown in the north tend to have less flavour – whether fresh or dried – than those grown in the south. You should bear this in mind when you are using herbs.

Chapter 4

SALTING

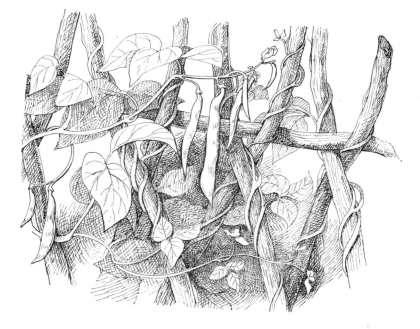

The use of salt dates back to the neolithic age, when natural deposits throughout Europe, north Africa and Asia minor were first exploited. It was quickly found to have many useful properties particularly as a preservative of animal tissue. However its use has largely been confined to meat and fish, and it is less suitable when applied directly to vegetable tissue. This is probably due to the actual structure and chemistry of these tissues compared with the cellular material of meat and fish. While salt is very important in the preservation of fruit and vegetables it is normally used with some other preservative such as vinegar, but there are a few vegetables, for example some varieties of beans and cabbage, which can be preserved by salting alone.

Brining on the other hand has been widely used. This is really a variant of pickling, and was used a great deal in Roman times. The main disadvantage of brining is that the preserves do not keep for long. This is due to the low concentration of salt used; a higher concentration would improve the keeping qualities of the preserve, but would also make it virtually unpalatable. In England this technique of 'pickling' has never been used to any great extent; we tend to prefer vinegar and wine as preservatives. But there is a strong tradition of brining in East European and Russian cookery.

For dry salting you must use the correct type of salt, so it is worth mentioning and distinguishing between the various types available.

Rock salt: salt mines were discovered near Northwich in Cheshire around 1670, and subsequently at other centres such as Nantwich and Droitwich. The rock salt was hewn out manually to begin with, but later it was dissolved and pumped out of the pits as brine, which was then evaporated in iron pans. Rock salt can be bought as unrefined crystals or, in a more refined state but without the addition of any other chemicals, as 'block' or 'kitchen' salt.

Sea salt: sea salt is obtained by the evaporation of sea water using artificial heat. There were important salt workings along the East Anglian and south coasts many of which are mentioned in the Domesday Book. The East Anglian works in particular played an important role in the development of the herring industry in the early middle ages. The well-known but rather costly Maldon salt is sea salt produced from the ancient workings at Maldon in Essex.

Bay salt: this is similar to sea salt. It is produced from sea water, but there is one important difference in the means of evaporation. Bay salt is formed by a slow process of natural evaporation using only the heat of the sun. The speed of evaporation affects both the size of the salt crystals and also their purity, and bay salt is considered to be the best quality salt for use in preserving because of its purity. Bay salt was named after Bourgneuf Bay around Noirmoutiers at the mouth of the River Loire. By the late middle ages this had become the most famous

34

salt-producing centre in Europe as a result of its unique position and geography. It was known throughout the medieval world simply as 'the Bay'. Most bay salt is now produced around the Mediterranean.

Table salt: this is highly refined salt usually produced from the old salt springs of Cheshire and Worcestershire. To prevent it forming lumps, magnesium carbonate is added to give it free-running qualities. Because of this, and also because it does not have a good flavour, it should not be used for dry salting.

Dry Salting

When dry salting vegetables you can use either rock, sea or bay salt. In terms of cost, block or kitchen salt is the cheapest, and is perfectly adequate for the process.

1. Be sure to use sufficient salt. The usual proportion is 1 lb. of kitchen salt to 3 lb. beans or other vegetables. The most common cause of failure is the use of too little salt. There is a tendency with grated block salt to use too little and with dense vacuum pack salt to use too much.

2. All the vegetables used should be young, fresh and tender, without blemishes or signs of decay.

3. When filling a jar with vegetables and salt in layers, press down firmly to ensure that there are no pockets of air trapped. Similarly as the salt and moisture from the vegetables combine to form a strong brine, do not throw it away, since this will also result in the formation of air pockets, where bacteria can develop.

4. If you are using a stoneware jar, do not stand it on stone, brick or concrete floors as moisture will be drawn up.

5. If the vegetables become slimy or decay, it is usually because too little salt has been added, or the whole was not pressed down sufficiently.

Brining

Brining has much in common with pickling except that the vegetables are preserved in a solution of salt, rather than in vinegar. Many of the rules for pickling also apply to brining (see pp. 58–9).

It is important to use a sufficient concentration of salt (usually 2 oz. per pint of water) and to ensure that the vegetables are completely covered.

Vegetables in brine do not keep for more than a few weeks and should be used up quickly.

Salted French and Runner Beans
3 lb. beans; 1 lb. kitchen salt.

Choose young, fresh beans; wash them and string if necessary. If they are small they can be left whole; if large runners they should be sliced.

Find a large earthenware jar and put about 1 inch of salt in the bottom. Then put on a layer of beans. Continue to fill the jar in layers. It is important to press the beans well down as you proceed; this is to get rid of any air pockets that might harbour bacteria and moulds. Finish the jar with a layer of salt. Then cover and leave for several days. During this time the beans will shrink and the jar can then be topped up with further layers of salt and beans, ensuring that there is always a layer of salt at the top of the jar.

You will notice that the salt gradually turns to brine; this should not be thrown away.

Cover the jar with a cloth or paper tied well down and store it in a dark, dry cupboard.

In theory salted beans should keep through the winter, but the process of salting is not always completely reliable, so in practice you should check the beans occasionally during storage, to make sure that they are not spoiling.

When you require some of the beans for cooking, take them out of the jar and wash them thoroughly to remove any excess salt and brine. (Put a layer of salt on top of the remaining beans and re-cover the jar.) Then soak the beans for 1 hour in warm water, strain and cook in un-salted water for about $\frac{1}{4}$ hour or until the beans are tender.

Salted Cabbage
Centuries ago the Chinese preserved cabbage by soaking it in rice wine; this method was adapted by Ghenghis Khan's invaders who substituted brine for rice wine; they carried the recipe with them and it travelled

westward, eventually reappearing in a modified form as German sauerkraut.

1 lb. cabbage; ½ oz. salt; a few caraway seeds.

Choose a hard white cabbage, wash and remove the outer leaves and stalk. Put a few of these leaves at the bottom of a large jar or wooden tub. Shred the rest of the cabbage and mix well with the salt and caraway seeds. Pack into your container, pressing down hard. Put a few whole leaves on top and then cover. It is important to have an arrangement so that the cover itself is weighted down and rests directly on the cabbage and all air is excluded.

Leave the container in this state for several weeks in a warm atmosphere (70–80°F). During this time the cabbage ferments and a strong brine solution is formed. It may be necessary to add a little more brine to bring the level up to the cover once more; use 1 oz. salt per quart of water.

When fermentation ceases, after 2–3 weeks, the cabbage is ready for use.

Note: A small quantity of salt is used deliberately to allow the cabbage to ferment. The same principle is involved in the preparation of certain 'semi-preserved' fish such as 'surstromming' – Swedish fermented herring.

Mushrooms in Brine
Use small button mushrooms for brining. Remove the stalks and wipe the flaps with a damp cloth. Then make up the brine.

For ½ lb. mushrooms use:
2 oz. salt; 2 pieces root ginger; 4 blades mace; 10 black peppercorns; 1 pint water.

Put the spices in a muslin bag and boil all the ingredients together for 10 minutes. Add the mushrooms and scald for 2 minutes. Then remove them and pack into jars; let the brine get cool, and pour it over the mushrooms until they are completely covered. Seal the jars and store.

They do not keep for very long since the concentration of salt is rather low; but the quantities needed for long keeping would make the mushrooms unpalatable. If you want to store the mushrooms for a longer period, pickle them in vinegar (see pp. 61–2). Brined mushrooms should be used up a few weeks after bottling.

Tomatoes in Brine

3 lb. tomatoes; 4 sprigs dill; 12 peppercorns; 1 clove garlic; 4 oz. salt; 2 pints water.

Choose small ripe tomatoes that are approximately the same size. Wash them and pack into jars. Put the sprigs of dill among them.

Then boil up the salt and water with the peppercorns and chopped garlic. Heat for 10 minutes then allow the solution to cool before pouring it over the tomatoes, making sure they are completely immersed. It is a good idea to put a few vine leaves on top of them.

Seal the jars well and store for a week or so before using.

A similar method can be used for cucumbers. These should be young and firm, and in this case vine leaves should be put at the bottom of the jar and at the top. These help to preserve the cucumbers and prevent them from going soft.

Both tomatoes and cucumbers in brine are best used a week after bottling, and they do not keep satisfactorily for more than a few weeks.

Chapter 5

PRESERVING IN SYRUP

The Romans were familiar with sugar in medicine, but did not use it at all in cookery; their most important sweetener and preservative was honey, and this was used extensively for preserving fruit. For instance, Columella mentions a method of preserving quinces in which the fruit was put into a wide-necked flagon, covered with willow twigs and then filled up with the best and most fluid honey. Similar methods were employed for preserving pears, apricots, grapes and service-berries.

The use of honey continued for a very long time, and it was not until the middle ages that sugar began to be accepted as a sweetener and a preservative. It was introduced into Britain mainly as a result of the Crusades; soldiers returning home spoke enthusiastically about sugar cane, and once interest was aroused sugar became part of the cargo of the spice ships that relayed goods from the Middle East to Europe and

Britain. However it was an expensive commodity that only the rich could afford, and its use was confined to special dishes for special occasions such as weddings and court banquets. The marriage of Henry IV to Joan of Navarre in 1403 was such an occasion, and the menu for that feast has references to 'perys in syrippe'. The pears eaten at this celebration were probably prepared using a similar recipe to that listed in the Harleian Manuscript 4016 dating from about 1450:

Take Wardons, and cast hem in a fair potte, and boil hem til their ben tendre; and take hem uppe, and pare hem in two or three. And take powder of Cannell [cinnamon], a good quantite, and cast hit in good red wyne, And cast sugar thereto, and put hit in an erthen potte, And lete boile; And then cast the peris thereto, And late hem boile togidre awhile; take powder of ginger, And a litell saffron to colloure hit with, And loke that hit be poynante and also doucet.

The 'Wardons' mentioned were Warden pears; these were very large and much harder than a normal pear so that boiling and steeping in syrup was the only way to make them edible.

Gradually sugar superseded honey as a preservative and sweetener, and by the end of the sixteenth century few recipes still listed honey for these purposes. At the same time there was an upsurge of interest in fruit; many large houses had extensive orchards, new varieties were introduced from abroad, and market gardening was established principally by immigrant French gardeners. The list of fruit grown in England by the middle of the seventeenth century included apples, pears, cherries, plums, gooseberries, strawberries, peaches, quinces and medlars. Many of these were preserved by strewing with sugar in layers, and then steaming in a dish over a boiling pot.

By the middle of the eighteenth century, large estates were almost self-sufficient, providing their own meat, fish, game, vegetables, and as Mathew Bramble indicates in Smollett's novel *Humphry Clinker*, 'all the different fruits which England may call her own'. One feature of gardening at this time was the emphasis on exotic fruit like nectarines and peaches; these were known as 'brandy fruit' since they were preserved in jars with a mixture of brandy and sugar syrup. Other fruit were simply boiled in syrup which was then reduced to a thick consistency and poured over the fruit in stoneware jars.

These rich preserves were maintained as special items prepared on a small scale in the kitchens of middle- and upper-class families who could afford sugar, brandy and spices and who could either grow or purchase fruit in quantity. Yet even Eliza Acton considered that these 'wet preserves' were costly and impractical unless used on a large scale. They tended to be 'lusciously sweet' due to the large quantities of sugar included in the hope of preserving the product for a long time. Because of this she suggested that the preserves should be drained and the fruit dried, and many of her recipes provide the option of leaving the fruit in syrup, or subsequently drying it.

Because of these factors – the cost, the quality of the product and its limited practical applications, preserved fruit of this type has never made a great impact on the eating habits of any section of the population, and this remains true today, but they are still worth making occasionally on a small scale as they can make marvellous desserts covered with whipped cream.

Important points in preserving:

1. Choose fruit that is just ripe, before it begins to feel soft. The harder fruits such as plums, pears, apricots or peaches are best as they tend to retain their shape and texture. Strawberries, raspberries and the like are less successful.

2. The fruit should be wiped with a damp cloth, rather than washed in copious quantities of water. It may be necessary to prick fruits such as plums with a needle.

3. After the fruit has been steeped in sugar, it should be packed into jars and completely covered with syrup. At this stage additional flavours such as brandy can be added.

4. The jars should be well sealed, either with plastic caps or corks dipped in wax. Once opened these fruits do not keep for long, so it is best to make small batches at a time. A longer life can be ensured by sterilizing the jars as for fruit syrups or ketchups (see p. 110).

Hamburgh Grapes Preserved Whole
This recipe dates from the middle of the nineteenth century although it it is likely that a similar preserve was made a century earlier. Hamburgh grapes are a type of black dessert grape.

Pick out some handsome little bunches, wipe them very carefully with soft old linen moistened with spirits and water, place them in a wide jar, and allow one ounce of white sugar candy beaten small to each pound of grapes, which, as the fruit is placed, must be scattered equally amongst it. Fill the jar up with French brandy, the best, and seeing in two days afterwards that the fruit is properly covered, make up safely with bladder and leather, and store away in a cool airy room.

The Art & Mystery of Curing, Potting and Preserving,
by A Wholesale Curer of Comestibles, Chapman &
Hall, 1864

Preserved Greengages

1 lb. greengages; 1 lb. sugar.

Choose greengages that are large, fully ripe and of good quality. Take off any stalks and weigh. Then put the fruit into a saucepan of water, bring to the boil and scald. Remove the greengages and put on a cloth to drain; then peel them carefully. Put the fruit into a bowl and strew with an equal weight of sugar. Leave overnight. Next day transfer both fruit and sugar to a preserving pan and simmer for about 5 minutes until a syrup is formed. Repeat this process once a day for 3 successive days. Then carefully lift the greengages out of the syrup and put them into jars; boil up the syrup once more, allow it to cool and then pour it over the fruit. Cover and store in a dry place.

This makes 'an elegant and very rich preserve'.

Preserved Quinces

2 lb. quinces; 2 lb. sugar; juice of 1 orange

Peel, core and cut the quinces into slices. Put these in a pan with enough water to cover them, and simmer until they begin to feel soft. Put the sugar into a bowl and warm it in the oven, then add it and the orange juice to the fruit and stir until dissolved. Simmer for another 10 minutes.

Remove the quinces and put them into jars. Then boil up the syrup until it is thick and pour it hot over the fruit. Cover and store.

This preserve should be used up fairly quickly as it does not keep for a long time.

Preserved Apricots

Choose large ripe apricots and wipe the skins with a damp cloth. It is sometimes suggested that you should remove the stones from the fruit, either by slitting the flesh, or by pushing the stone out through the stalk end with a suitable instrument. But we find it is best to keep the fruit intact; the less damage done to it the better. Weigh the apricots and for each pound of fruit allow 1 lb. of sugar. Put them into a shallow dish and strew with half the sugar. Leave for 24 hours.

Next day transfer the apricots and syrup to a saucepan, bring to the boil, stirring in the remainder of the sugar. Continue to simmer for 10 minutes. Test the apricots. If they feel soft and have a bright appearance they are ready for bottling, if not they should be boiled up for a further 10 minutes. Then put the fruit into glass jars, pour the syrup over them and cover well.

Preserved Cherries

1 lb. Morello cherries; 1½ lb. sugar; ¼ pint redcurrant juice (strained).

Since this recipe requires redcurrant juice, it is best made in conjunction with redcurrant jelly. Cook the currants in the normal way with water (see redcurrant jelly recipe p. 138) and after straining, use some of the juice for your preserved cherries.

Choose cherries that are fully ripe, remove the stalks and wipe with a damp cloth. Prick the fruit with a needle in one or two places and put in a bowl. For each pound of fruit allow 1½ lb. of sugar, and strew half of this over the cherries. Leave for a day. Put the rest of the sugar into a saucepan and add redcurrant juice until it is dissolved; then boil for 10–15 minutes. After skimming this syrup, add the cherries (with their sugar) and simmer for 5 minutes. Carefully take out the cherries and put them into jars; boil up the syrup once more and pour it cool over the fruit. Cover and store in a dry dark cupboard.

Preserved Oranges

6 oranges; 1½ lb. sugar; ¼ pint dry white wine.

You must use oranges that are thin-skinned, firm and sweet, and preferably not too large. Wipe the skins with a damp cloth and then cut

43

the oranges into slices less than $\frac{1}{4}$ inch thick. Do not use the outer slices that contain no flesh, and remove all pips. Put the slices into a shallow dish and cover with the sugar. Allow to stand overnight.

Next day put the syrup and the oranges into a pan, bring to the boil and then simmer until the slices are tender. You may need to add a little water if you find the syrup is becoming too thick. The slices should have a clear appearance after cooking. Just before removing the pan from the heat pour in the white wine and stir gently. Transfer the oranges and syrup to wide-mouthed glass jars and seal. The oranges should set as rounds in a thin jelly.

Preserved Damsons

Choose large ripe damsons and remove their stalks. Do not use any that are bruised or blemished. Put them into a pan with just enough water to cover them, and simmer for 10 minutes. Do not heat too quickly or the skins will split. Lift out the damsons and drain them carefully. Weigh out 1 lb. of sugar for every pound of fruit; strew one half of this over the damsons in a dish, and add the other half to the water in which the damsons were boiled. Heat this up, bring to the boil and simmer for 10 minutes. You may need to skim the syrup as it boils. Allow this syrup and the damsons to stand overnight.

Next day add the damsons to the pan with the syrup and simmer for 30 minutes. Then lift out the fruit and pack into jars. Simmer the syrup for a further 30 minutes and pour it over the fruit. Cover well.

As it cools the syrup should turn almost to a jelly in which the damsons are suspended.

Preserved Tomatoes

3 lb. tomatoes; juice and rind of 2 lemons; 2 blades mace; 2 pieces root ginger; sugar.

Use tomatoes that are orange in colour but not quite ripe. Put them into a pan with enough water to cover them. Tie the mace, ginger and pieces of lemon rind in a muslin bag and allow the whole to simmer slowly for about 15 minutes. Then carefully remove the tomatoes and put them to drain; also take out the muslin bag. Add the lemon juice to the water with sufficient sugar to make a thin syrup (8 oz. for every pint of water). When the sugar has dissolved, bring the syrup to the boil. Meanwhile transfer the tomatoes to a shallow dish and pour the hot syrup over them. Leave for 4 days.

Then strain off the syrup, put it into a saucepan and add some more sugar (another 4 oz. per pint or sufficient to make a thick syrup). Add the tomatoes and simmer for 15 minutes and leave for another 4 days. By this time the syrup should have completely penetrated the tomatoes, so remove them and pack carefully into jars, boil up the syrup once more and pour it hot over the fruit. Cover and store in a dry place.

Preserved Walnuts

It was the custom during the seventeenth and eighteenth centuries to pick walnuts for preserving and pickling at the first full moon after midsummer. Later, when the links between plants, ritual and superstition weakened, the fruits were picked simply when they were green and before the shell had begun to form; in this case it seems that botanical science and superstition agree, for walnuts are still picked in late June for preserving.

Take a quantity of green walnuts, and find a jar that will easily contain them. Put a layer of sugar in the bottom of the jar about $\frac{1}{2}$ inch thick and then place a layer of walnuts on this. Continue to fill the jar layer by layer finishing off with sugar at the top. You should aim to use $\frac{1}{2}$ lb. of sugar for each pound of nuts.

Cover the jar loosely and put into a pan of water. Bring this slowly to the boil and let it simmer for 3 hours. During this time you may need to top up with water occasionally so that the level remains fairly constant – about 2 inches from the top of the jar. The sugar is melted by the heat of the water, and forms a syrup with the liquid that is extracted from the nuts. If this syrup does not completely cover the nuts, add more sugar and continue to simmer. Then remove the jar from the water carefully, let it get cold, and cover well. This preserve should be stored for a few months before using.

These will be found of extensive and excellent use in families of many children as a gentle aperient medicine. One is a dose for a child of five to seven years old, and so in advancing ratio, and instead of proving nauseous to young palates, will be regarded as a treat and, if I am not mistaken, adults will occasionally be troubled with constipation.

> *The Art & Mystery of Curing, Potting and Preserving,*
> by A Wholesale Curer of Comestibles, Chapman &
> Hall, 1864

Preserved Cucumbers

1 lb. cucumber; 1 lb. sugar; 1 pint water; rind of 1 lemon; 2 pieces root ginger.

For this recipe you need small immature cucumbers with few pips. First scald them in a pan of boiling water for a few minutes and then drain and prick each cucumber with a needle in several places. While the cucumbers are draining, put the sugar and water together in a saucepan and simmer gently until the sugar is dissolved. Add the lemon rind, ginger and cucumbers and bring the syrup to the boil. Then turn down the heat and allow it to simmer for another 5 minutes. Take out the cucumbers, pack into clean jars and then pour the strained syrup over them, making sure they are completely covered. Leave for 4 days.

Drain the syrup, boil it up again, and pour it hot over the cucumbers. Repeat this process once more after 4 days. Finally seal the jars well and store.

If during storage you notice any signs of fermentation, such as bubbles of gas in the syrup, strain and boil up again.

Preserved Lettuce Stalks

If you grow lettuces in your garden, particularly the upright cos variety, you can use the stalks from any plants that run to seed. First strip the stalks and peel off the outer fibrous sheath; the inner core is what you will need for preserving. Chop into pieces and weigh. Then weigh out an equal quantity of sugar.

Put the sugar and a few pieces of root ginger into a pan with enough water to contain and cover the pieces of lettuce stalk. Boil up the syrup and then add the stalks. Remove from the heat and leave overnight. Next day drain off the syrup, boil it up once more and pour it over the stalks. Let it stand for a day. Repeat this operation until the stems look clear and the syrup has thickened. During the final boiling of the syrup,

add the juice of a lemon, and then pack the stalks into jars and cover with the syrup.

One writer has likened this preserve to Chinese ginger.

47

Preserved Eryngo Root

Eryngo, or sea holly, once a common and widely used seashore plant, is now very scarce, and we do not encourage people to dig up any specimens that they find. For preserving the roots were boiled and the outer skin removed; they were then cooked in syrup and bottled, perhaps with the addition of rosewater, cinnamon and musk. The root was also candied, and an important local industry, established in Colchester at the end of the sixteenth century, survived until Victorian times. In this form, eryngo was an essential ingredient of marrow-bone pie, and was also used with orchid tubers and a potent combination of herbs and spices in an infamous seventeenth-century aphrodisiac.

The woody portions of the root were dried and used rather like cinnamon sticks.

As well as eryngo, many other roots of wild plants were preserved in syrup: these included elecampane, fennel and alexanders.

PART TWO

Chapter 6

PICKLES AND
FLAVOURED VINEGARS

PICKLES

Pickling is one of the most ancient methods of preserving fruit and vegetables. Both the Greeks and the Romans made use of it, and the Romans in particular developed the craft of pickling to a very high degree. The Roman aristocracy enjoyed a great variety of pickles and cured meats, which were imported from their conquered territories in Europe; and from north Africa and the Middle East they obtained plums, lemons, peaches and apricots, some of which were undoubtedly made into pickles. In addition to fruit they made pickles from herbs,

51

roots, flowers and vegetables: both Apicius and Columella mention ways of pickling onions, plums, lettuce leaves, turnips (these were preserved in a pickle made from honey, myrtle berries and vinegar), asparagus, fennel, charlock and cabbage stalks. And in the *Satyricon*, Petronius even mentions pickled cumin seeds. The ingredients were normally macerated in a mixture of oil, brine and vinegar, which was added carefully drop by drop, and the pickles were stored for a long time in large cylindrical vases. It's curious that this delicate and sophisticated approach to the preparation of food existed alongside the ridiculous over-indulgence that characterized the eating habits of the ruling classes of Imperial Rome.

After the fall of the Roman Empire the main centres of cookery in Europe were the monasteries. The monks cultivated extensive herb and vegetable gardens and orchards, and the monasteries themselves were equipped with special rooms for brewing, baking and preserving. By the eleventh century these skills were again being used widely and many large households could boast of extensive kitchens, gardens, and cellars stocked with wine, vinegar and verjuice (the juice extracted from sour crab apples, although the word also refers to grape juice in this period). However it is likely that these were used mainly in cooking, especially in the preparation of sauces. Pickling itself was fairly limited during the early medieval period because there were few vegetables available; onions, leeks, root crops and cabbages are the most often mentioned. One of the few specific references to pickles comes in a household list of 1290, which mentions 'pickled greens' (probably cabbages). Fruit was also confined to a few varieties, most of which was either imported dried, or preserved with honey.

In 1393, the 'Goodman of Paris', a wealthy but unnamed merchant, wrote a book of instruction to his young bride. At the time he was sixty years old and she was fifteen, and throughout the book, in true courtly fashion, he addresses her as 'sister'. He tells her how to pickle rose buds in grape verjuice, not for eating, but to preserve their colour, and he also mentions the many uses of cabbages, which were often eaten raw or mixed with herbs and vinegar. Such dishes were quite common at this time, and seem to have been mid-way between salads and pickles.

As the list of fruit and vegetables available to cooks increased through the fifteenth and sixteenth centuries, so the number of pickles also increased. In the sixteenth century in particular there was an emphasis on delicate pickles which were used to garnish salads. The Elizabethans cared a great deal about the appearance of their food, so they used flowers, both fresh and pickled, to give colour and scent to grand salads. They also used herbs extensively; this was a tradition carried over from the middle ages, when herbs had an important dual function as foods and medicines. The term 'herb' was then used quite generally to include not only the conventional flavouring herbs that we are familiar with, but also large numbers of wild plants and salad vegetables. Many of these were subsequently pickled to add flavours to salads and also for winter use when no fresh vegetables were available. By the seventeenth century, writers like Gervaise Markham, Robert May and John Evelyn were mentioning pickles made from broom buds, alexander buds, rock samphire, ash keys, and the leaves from young radishes, turnips and lettuce; mushrooms, cucumbers and walnuts were also pickled. It is worth noting that verjuice was still used a great deal for pickling in the seventeenth century, so many of the pickles were probably very mild with a slightly sharp cider flavour, compared with later products that used pungent malt vinegar.

Two interesting developments in pickling occurred in the eighteenth century. The first was the increasing use of fruit; colourful pickles were made from redcurrants, grapes and barberries, often using a liquor of wine or wine vinegar. Secondly, the influence of the East India Company's trade with the Orient meant that many new fruits were introduced, and this gave rise to a vogue for imitations. A number of different fruits and vegetables, including melons, cucumbers, peaches, plums and later marrows were turned into complicated pickles under the general title 'mangoes'. There were other imitations as well; young cauliflower stalks were made into 'mock ginger', and elder buds pickled in alegar (sour ale) were thought to resemble bamboo shoots.

The eighteenth century also saw the publication of the first of a line of books which covered in great detail the whole subject of cookery and domestic economy; these contained chapters on preserving, and listed a great many recipes for pickles. The first really important book of this type was *The Art of Cookery Made Plain and Easy* by Hannah Glasse (1747), which includes a lot of the pickles that are quite familiar –

onions, beetroot, red cabbage, gherkins and so on. But there are still a number of rarities like pickled asparagus, fennel, two ways of pickling artichokes (one using the young leaves, the other the artichoke bottoms), radish pods, samphire and barberries. These are really the descendants of the Elizabethan style of pickling, and since the eighteenth century they have slowly disappeared from cookery books. Hannah Glasse's pickles were a great deal more pungent than their predecessors; she makes no mention of verjuice, and almost invariably uses wine vinegar as the liquor. She also tends to include large quantities of spices such as horseradish, mustard seed and ginger.

The trend started by books like *The Art of Cookery* culminated in the publication in 1845 of Eliza Acton's *Modern Cookery for Private Families*, the true forerunner of modern cookery books. Her list of pickles is quite short but it is the instructions themselves that make the book so important. They are precise, accurate and obviously written from trial and experience. They list quantities of ingredients and techniques in great detail and expose many of the pitfalls and problems that often beset pickling. Eliza Acton had a firm belief in the virtues of home-cooking and she was very critical of the commercial pickle-makers and their products which had begun to appear in London:

With the exception of walnuts, which when softened by keeping, or by the mode of preparing them, are the least objectionable of any pickle, with Indian Mangoes, and one or two other varieties these are not very wholesome articles of diet, consisting, as so many of them do, of crude hard vegetables, or of unripe fruit. In numerous instances, too, those which are commonly sold to the public have been found of so deadly a nature as to be eminently dangerous to persons who partake of them often and largely. It is most desirable, therefore, to have them prepared at home, and with good 'genuine' vinegar, whether French or English. That which is home-made can at least be relied on; and it may be made of excellent quality and of sufficient strength for all ordinary purposes.

Modern Cookery for Private Families, Eliza Acton, 1845

The reference to 'genuine' vinegar seems to indicate that Eliza Acton was aware of the problem of adulteration. In particular she may well have known about the work done during the last half of the eighteenth century by the chemist H. Jackson. He drew attention to the practice of adding copper salts to improve the colour of green vegetables;

pickles were deliberately made in copper vessels, so that a fresh-looking, but deadly, green colour was produced by the action of the vinegar on the copper. He warned against the use of earthenware vessels for pickling because of the danger of lead from the glaze being dissolved by the vinegar – something that even today is a hazard where lead glazes are still used. Jackson's curiosity also led him to identify the main ingredients in much commercially used vinegar. He found that it was often composed of a dilute solution of sulphuric acid, coloured with burnt sugar or infusions of oak-chips.

In the latter half of the nineteenth century more and more firms began to manufacture pickles, and while adulteration was a problem to begin with, it was alleviated by the natural growth of the food industry, which tended to discourage the unscrupulous back street manufacturer, and also by laws which resulted from a special government inquiry into food adulteration carried out in 1899. Today's pickle manufacturers have grown up from the small number of firms established at the end of the nineteenth century. Of course there have been many changes; we no longer have the same fear of chemical adulteration although sophisticated food 'additives' are adulterants in their own right and may yet turn out to be as dangerous as the simple poisons of the nineteenth century. The range of pickles offered is also very different; there are still onions, red cabbage and walnuts, but what about damsons, mushrooms and radish pods? This is partly due to the popular appeal of some pickles, and also to the fact that many of the less well known types have simply gone out of fashion.

Vinegar

The Roman writer Columella states quite plainly that 'vinegar and hard brine are essential for making preserves'. The word is derived from the French *vin aigré* meaning sour wine, and in Roman times this is what vinegar was made from. Yeast, dried figs, salt and honey were added to give a product that was used in food preservation and also as a drink diluted with water. Wine vinegar remained popular right up to the nineteenth century although it was gradually superseded by malt vinegar. At first, malt vinegar was often of dubious quality and contained adulterants. Because of this, most discerning cooks continued to use wine vinegar, or to make their own from safe ingredients. Nowadays of course both dark, malt vinegar and white or distilled vinegar are relatively cheap and of good quality. It is important to use the best vinegar for preserving since the content of acetic acid is the critical factor that determines the effectiveness of the vinegar as a preservative. Most commercially sold vinegar except barrelled vinegar is required to have an acetic acid content of about 5 per cent which is quite suitable.

It may be useful to look at the various types of vinegar available today:

Malt vinegar: as its name implies, malt vinegar is formed by the fermentation of malted barley, sometimes with cereal grain added. The starch in these raw materials is converted to sugars which are fermented to give alcohol and finally acetic acid. Malt vinegar is the cheapest and most widely used vinegar for pickles. It does have a strong pungent taste, but this is important for a number of pickles like eggs and onions. Often the vinegar is subsequently spiced; this is a matter of personal taste, but we find that some pickles really do need fiery spices like black peppercorns, chillies, and ginger, whereas eggs, for instance, are dulled by spicing. We have tasted eggs pickled with cinnamon and ginger, and the flavours simply do not blend.

White (distilled) vinegar: this is merely vinegar made by distilling malt vinegar. It is colourless, has a smoother, less pungent taste and is useful where a mild pickle is required. Because it is colourless it is good for pickling red cabbage, cucumber, French beans etc.; the vinegar enhances the colour of vegetables and gives the pickle an attractive appearance.

Spirit vinegar: this is vinegar made by fermenting molasses. It is not normally available in shops, but is used commercially for the manufacture of pickles since it has a very high acetic acid content – usually 10–13 per cent. This is why most factory-made pickles are very acidic and sharp tasting.

Wine vinegar: this results from the fermentation of the sugar in grapes to give alcohol, which is in turn fermented to form acetic acid. However it is usually made directly from wine. This vinegar is relatively expensive nowadays, but it is the best one to use in those pickles for which malt vinegar would be too pungent. It gives the pickle a characteristic delicate flavour and suits vegetables like asparagus and mushrooms very well.

Cider vinegar: this uses apples as its starting material. It is also quite expensive but is good in some pickles, for example samphire. A satisfactory imitation can be made by mixing equal quantities of cider and distilled vinegar.

There are a number of other types of vinegar such as herb vinegars, fruit-flavoured vinegars, verjuice, and vinegars made from fruit wines. These are all mentioned under Flavoured Vinegars on pp. 86–93.

The choice of vinegar will depend on several factors, first the actual fruit or vegetable that you are pickling, also the colour and appearance of the pickle, and the flavour and overall effect you want to achieve. If spices are added, they should be boiled in the vinegar for about 10 minutes; they can either be tied in a muslin bag or left free. Some pickles are best made by pouring hot vinegar over the main ingredient e.g. plums, walnuts; this gives a soft texture. With crisp vegetables like cucumber and red cabbage use vinegar that has been allowed to cool after boiling.

Salt

This is an essential preservative. Fruit and vegetables are either steeped in brine or strewn with dry salt before pickling. The action of salt is quite complex, but involves the drawing out of moisture from the tissues of the fruit or vegetables. In large-scale processes, the steeping in brine continues over a long period; in fact vegetables are stored this way until ready for pickling, consequently the tissues become hard and rubbery, lose their crispness, and the pickle tastes extremely salty. At home, this process should only continue for about 24 hours.

When using brine you should take 2 oz. cooking salt per pint of water. In many old recipes there are instructions to put the vegetables in water with sufficient salt 'to bear or float an egg'. This is a system based on trial and experience – in fact it gives a slightly more concentrated brine than the 2 oz. per pint used nowadays. But it is still convenient where large amounts of water are needed – it saves measuring out quantities in advance.

The use of brine or dry salt depends on the type of material being pickled. If you want a very crisp product, then dry salt is best, but remember to wash off any excess before finally pickling.

Points to remember in pickling are:

1. Always use fresh, good quality fruit and vegetables for pickling. Discard any that are discoloured, over-ripe or blemished.

2. Use good quality vinegar.

3. Don't use copper, brass or iron pans when making pickles. Eliza Acton gives a horrifying description of the way pickle manufacturers exploited the green colour of copper compounds produced by the action of vinegar on brass:

> The gherkins thus pickled are very crisp, and excellent in flavour, and the colour is sufficiently good to satisfy the prudent housekeeper, to whom the brilliant and *poisonous* green produced by boiling the vinegar in a brass skillet (a process constantly recommended in books of cookery) is anything but attractive. To satisfy ourselves of the effect produced by the action of the acid on metal, we had a few gherkins thrown into some vinegar which was boiling in a brass pan, and nothing could be more beautiful than the colour which they almost immediately exhibited. We fear this dangerous method is too often resorted to in preparing pickles for sale.
>
> *Modern Cookery for Private Families*, Eliza Acton, 1845

You will be safe enough if you use an aluminium, stainless steel or enamel-lined pan, and pack the pickles in glass jars.

4. Always make sure the vegetables are completely covered with the vinegar when they are bottled.

5. The pickle should be well covered. A great variety of covers was used in the past, such as writing paper soaked in brandy, or 'scere-cloth' – where jars were sealed by being tied down with waxed cloth. The space between the preserve and the cover was often filled with melted paraffin wax or mutton fat. The principle of covering with paraffin wax is still used in America. There are a number of methods available today:

A. Metal or plastic caps with a vinegar-proof lining. This ensures that there is no contact between the vinegar and the metal. It is the most useful, and really the most practical way of covering pickles since, as the pickle is used, the cap can be taken off and replaced quite easily.

B. Greaseproof paper and then a round of muslin dipped in melted paraffin wax or fat. This is an effective seal when made correctly. It might be useful where the pickle is stored in stoneware jars rather than glass.

C. You can buy rolls of preserving skin which can be used to cover the jars.

Special pickling jars can be got in some places, but this isn't really worthwhile, as they are relatively expensive, and a supply of free glass jars is always easy to come by.

Remember that pickles which have a long life, such as onions, can be made in large batches, whilst others, such as red cabbage, or cucumbers should be made in small quantities at intervals; so you will need to decide the size of jar you require for a particular pickle, otherwise you will be left with half a jar of soggy, vinegar-soaked vegetables which is quite useless. The size of the jar will also depend on the quantity of pickle that you are likely to consume.

6. Pickles should be stored in a cool dry, place, preferably in a dark cupboard. Don't forget to label the jar before storing with its type and the date it was made. The length of time during which pickles are stored is very important. They do not keep indefinitely although some have a useful shelf life of up to a year. But there's normally an optimum period during which the pickle is at its best, after this its quality deteriorates. We have indicated in the recipes where these times are most critical.

Pickled Onions

Early memories of pickled onions have determined most of my present attitudes towards them. It's a sad fact that so many really magnificent foods like marrow, turnips, stew and rice pudding have been lost to us, simply because memories of those tasteless masses served up at school and at seaside boarding houses seem to be indelibly stamped on our collective palate. Pickled onions fit into this category as well – they're good props for music-hall jokes, but as a food to be taken seriously they're hardly considered. We expect a soggy, vinegar-soaked globe, and we normally get just that.

Unlike Rose, I was brought up on pickled onions and chutneys purchased from the local grocer, and every Monday lunchtime a whole tray of assorted jars would appear on the table to embellish cold beef, mashed swede and potatoes baked in their jackets. Although I helped myself to lavish quantities of chutney and mustard pickle I had an aversion to those sharp vinegary onions; it only disappeared when I discovered a fish and chip shop that sold its own home-made pickled onions. With cod and chips they were a revelation!

The term 'pickled onion' is rather a misnomer, since shallots are usually grown for pickling these days. You can still buy special pickling onions – the variety 'Small Paris Silver-Skin' grown from seed is recommended. However, shallots are much more reliable and easy to grow, and they have a stronger flavour than onions. Traditionally shallots are planted on the shortest day and lifted on the longest, but nowadays with the shifts in seasonal conditions it's best to plant in February and lift in July. Wait until the leaves are yellow and drooping, then dig up the shallots on a dry, sunny day. Don't attempt to pickle them straight away, but let them dry out, either in the sun or, if the weather is unreliable, in a warm, dry place indoors. Leave them until the outer skins have become brown, at which time you should put aside a proportion of your crop and store them. These shallots can be sown the following February; so once you have grown shallots for one season, you will not need to buy any more for sowing. When the shallots have dried out – usually in the early autumn, then you can begin to pickle them. These pickles will be ready for use at Christmas, which is the ideal occasion for a celebration of the skills of pickling and preserving; it's a surprising echo of that other 'harvest festival', and, indirectly at least, it is about the same things – a successful season, good produce, the full use of all one's resources, and the satisfaction of knowing that the pickle cupboard, like the barn, is full.

When your shallots are ready they must first be peeled. Be careful not to scar the tissue as this produces a dark blemish on the shallot when it is pickled, so remove only the minimum at the base and tip of each shallot. After peeling, soak them overnight in brine (2 oz. salt per pint of water). Next day wash them with cold water; this is important since the pickle will be excessively salty if the shallots aren't washed.

Meanwhile prepare the vinegar. We find it best to use highly spiced malt vinegar for this: a mixture of black peppercorns, root ginger, dried chillies, with a few coriander seeds and bay leaves will give you a very pungent pickle which certainly suits the flavour and texture of the shallots. Boil the vinegar with these spices for about 15 minutes and allow it to cool. Pack the shallots into glass jars and pour over the cold vinegar, making sure they are completely covered. Seal and store for a couple of months before using. They do keep their flavour and crispness up to 6 months after bottling, but are best after 2–3 months. It is worthwhile sampling the pickle at intervals, to check how it is maturing.

Because pickled onions have this pungency and crispness, it's best to eat them with quite simple foods. For years they have been eaten with bread and cheese, a tradition that has led to the development of that pitiful imitation 'the ploughman's lunch', served up delicately for hungry businessmen in country pubs and hotels. Originally the farm labourer's 'lunch' consisted of a huge hunk of bread, and a piece of cheese about the same size. This was called 'field fare'. Nowadays a minute portion of cheddar with a couple of slices of airy, insubstantial 'French' bread is the usual food offered. The whole style and emphasis of this meal has changed; it's become 'civilized' and it doesn't even perform its main function any longer – that of filling one's stomach. It was quite a different story years ago, when farm labourers gathered in the pub to celebrate the sheep-shearing:

. . . the table would be laden with a big round of salt beef, a ham and bread and cheese and pickled onions, and with fare like that in front of you, a couple or three golden sovereigns in your money pouch to take home to mother, what else would a man want to do but sing? The songs came thick and fast, for the more they sang the more they drank – every song a drink was the rule – and the more they drank the more they sang. . .
A Song for Every Season, Bob Copper, Heinemann, 1971

Pickled Mushrooms
You must use only the smallest button mushrooms, preferably meadow-picked, for pickling. These should be pure white with pale pink gills.

small button mushrooms; a few blades of mace; black peppercorns; white wine; wine vinegar.

Collect some button mushrooms, cut off the stalks level with the base of the mushroom 'head' and wipe with a damp cloth. Then put them into some boiling salted water (2 oz. salt per pint) for 5 minutes. Drain the mushrooms well and then put them into a mixture of wine vinegar, mace and peppercorns (4 blades of mace and 10 peppercorns for each pint of vinegar). Let the mushrooms steep for 24 hours. Then drain the mushrooms and pack into jars. Make up a mixture of equal quantities of wine vinegar and white wine; one writer suggests that 'the wine should be good old Madeira and the quantity may be increased with great advantage'. Cover and store for a couple of weeks before using. It is not worth trying to keep this pickle for a long time as the mushrooms will tend to deteriorate; so make it in small batches and use it quickly.

Pickled Kidney and Broad Beans
The original of this seventeenth-century recipe relates to kidney beans, but it can be quite easily adapted to suit broad beans. This is a good way of using up beans that have become large and tough skinned, and are no longer much good for eating fresh.

beans; cloves, mace, root ginger, black peppercorns; salt; peel of 1 orange; wine vinegar.

Gather the beans on a dry day, and shell and weigh them. Put them into salt water (about 2 tsp. salt per pound of beans), scald and cook gently until they are just beginning to feel soft. This is important – and you will have to test by biting into a sample bean during cooking. The skins must not be allowed to split; any beans that do should be discarded as they will break up in the pickle. Then strain the beans and allow them to cool.

Meanwhile put the vinegar to boil with the spices and orange peel. The original recipes state that you should use 'so much of these spices as will make ye pickle tast prety strong of it'. A useful mixture is 3 cloves, 2 blades of mace, 3 pieces of root ginger and 10 peppercorns for each pint of vinegar, but you can vary this according to your own taste.

When the vinegar has boiled for about 10 minutes, allow it to cool. Pack the beans carefully into jars and pour over the cold vinegar so that it completely covers them. Seal in the usual way and store for a couple of weeks before using.

Pickled French Beans

(1) 1 lb. green beans; ½ pint cider vinegar (or ¼ pint dry cider and ¼ pint white vinegar); ¼ lb. brown sugar; 2 tsp. dill seeds; ¼ tsp. turmeric; ¼ tsp. cayenne pepper.

Choose beans, either from your garden or from the shops, which are firm and fresh, and not too large. Top and tail them, and boil in salted water until they are tender, but still slightly crisp. Be careful not to overcook them, otherwise the beans will become mushy in the pickle. When they are cooked, drain well, and pack them whole into a large jar.

Meanwhile put all the other ingredients in a saucepan with the vinegar, and boil for 10 minutes. Then pour the hot, spiced vinegar over the beans, making sure they are completely covered, and seal the jar. You will need to leave this pickle about 2 months before it is ready.

(2) This is an eighteenth-century recipe.

Choose some young French beans and put them into a dish. Cover with boiling white wine and leave overnight. Next day strain off the wine. Make up a spiced vinegar of the following:

1 pint white wine vinegar; 1 tsp. Jamaica pepper (whole allspice); 2 tsp. black peppercorns; 4 pieces root ginger; 2 blades mace.

Boil the vinegar and spices together for 15 minutes. Strain and pour the hot vinegar over the beans. Leave overnight. Next day strain off the vinegar, re-boil and pour over the beans once again. Repeat this process for 2 or 3 days, until the beans look green. Then cover and store.

Pickled Celery

2 heads of celery; 2 tsp. salt; 1 green or red pepper; 4 pieces root ginger; 4 blades mace; 1 pint white vinegar.

When you are choosing celery, avoid the anaemic, cellophane-wrapped article that appears unnaturally out of season in many shops. Wait until November when boxes of dirty, sooty celery come on the market. Wash off the dirt and you will see that the stems are pure white with fresh green tops. This is the only celery worth eating and it makes a good pickle as well.

Choose two good heads and cut off the green tops. Wash the white parts well and divide them into sticks. Wipe them dry. Hollow out the pepper, discard the seeds, and cut lengthways into thin strips. Put the vinegar, salt and spices (in a muslin bag) into a large saucepan and boil for 10 minutes. Then toss in the sticks of celery and the strips of pepper. Continue boiling for 5 minutes only. Strain off the vinegar and remove the bag of spices. Pack the celery into jars keeping the sticks upright, and put strips of pepper among them. When the vinegar is cold, pour it over the celery making sure that it is completely covered. Seal the jars and store in a dry place. This is a pickle that should be eaten young, after a couple of weeks' storage. It goes well in winter salads and makes an interesting alternative to fresh celery with cheese, especially the solid English varieties.

When you have finished all the celery, re-bottle the vinegar and keep it for use.

Pickled Beetroot

Beetroot are grown primarily for use fresh, but you can pickle the small 'baby beets', which are the thinnings from the crop, and also the very large roots at the end of the season. The young beetroots can be pulled by hand when they are the right size for pickling whole, but at the end of the season you will probably need to dig up the large roots. In both cases it is important not to bruise them. Twist the leaves off by hand, leaving a little stalk, and wash but do not peel. Put them to boil in a saucepan of salted water until they are tender. Meanwhile boil up some white vinegar in another saucepan. If you like a strong pickle then you can add a few spices to the vinegar at this stage. A good recipe is the following:

½ tsp. cayenne pepper; 1 tsp. ground ginger; a few black peppercorns; 1 pint white vinegar.

When the beetroots are cooked, allow them to cool a little before peeling them. Put small ones whole into a wide-mouthed glass jar, and pour the cooled spiced vinegar over them so that they are completely covered. When you are pickling large, old beetroots, you will need to cut them into slices before pickling, and you can cut these slices into 'various ornamental and grotesque figures'.

This recipe will give you a good pickle with a fresh fiery taste. The white vinegar heightens the flavour of the beetroot, and also brings out its colour. The pickle is ready for use soon after it is made, but also keeps for a long time without deteriorating. Eat it with salads or cheese.

Pickled Jerusalem Artichokes

This is a simple but very effective pickle that enhances the special taste and texture of Jerusalem artichokes.

1 lb. Jerusalem artichokes; salt; 2 bay leaves; peel of 1 lemon; white vinegar.

Artichokes can usually be found in greengrocers' shops from November onwards. If you grow them, they should be dug up at this time. The most awkward part of this pickle is peeling the artichokes themselves; often they appear like warty potatoes, each tuber a mass of crevices and bumps. When you have peeled the artichokes, put them in salted water and cook until *just* tender (it is better to undercook them if you are in any doubt). Meanwhile remove the peel from a lemon, ensuring no pith is attached, and cut it into thin strips. Put these and the bay leaves into a pint of white vinegar and boil for 10 minutes. Strain and allow the vinegar to cool. (Don't throw away the lemon peel and bay leaves.) When the artichokes are cooked, drain them well and pack into jars, putting pieces of lemon peel and bay leaves among them. When the vinegar is cold pour it over the tubers, making sure they are completely covered, and seal in the usual way. They should be stored for a couple of weeks before using.

These artichokes are very good sliced as part of a winter salad or as an accompaniment to oily smoked sprats or smoked eel. The lemon, as well as giving the pickle colour, helps to counteract the fattiness of these foods without obscuring their delicate taste.

The vinegar left after all the artichokes have been eaten should be kept. It has a special and very unusual flavour.

Pickled Red Cabbage

After the first frosts of autumn, red cabbages are common and cheap in most greengrocers' shops, but wait until October before you buy any, since the quality of the cabbage is much improved after several frosts have 'seasoned' it. We always pickle red cabbage in small batches since it must be eaten when it is young and has that special blend of crispness, taste and colour which the factory-made pickle can never match.

Choose a weighty, close-knit cabbage and cut off any superfluous leaves; only the heart will make a good pickle. Chop the cabbage finely, but roughly, so that you have a variety of pieces, some leaf, some stalk, which will have different textures when pickled. Put the cabbage into a large dish, scatter cooking salt over it, and let it stand overnight.

Next day, wash the cabbage free of salt and let it drain in a sieve. Then pack into jars and cover with white vinegar which you have previously boiled and allowed to cool. (When packing the jars you may like to add a few bay leaves and black peppercorns with the cabbage, although we find that this does little to improve the flavour of the pickle.)

In a couple of weeks you will have an extraordinary pickle which bears almost no resemblance to the discoloured, soggy article that can be purchased in most shops. It should be bright red, crisp and sharp tasting. One friend of ours, alone in her cottage, can, and does, consume a whole jar, unaccompanied, at one sitting. Those who made the pickle in the last century were quick to recognize its special characteristics, and one even described it as 'perhaps the best article of its kind to be found anywhere, its excellency consisting in its flavour, its colour and its crispness'.

Pickled Lemons

1 lb. lemons; 3 tbs. salt; 1 tsp. tumeric; $\frac{1}{2}$ tsp. cayenne pepper; 2 tsp. ground allspice; white vinegar.

Choose several good size lemons, wipe them with a damp cloth, and cut the fruit into chunks, removing the pips. Do this on a plate or in a bowl to catch as much of the juice as possible. Then pack the fruit into a screw-top jar. Put the spices and salt in the bowl with a little vinegar and mix with the juice of the lemons. Add this solution to the lemons in the jar and top up with vinegar, so that the fruit is completely covered. Give the jar a good shake and leave it in a warm place by a window if the weather is sunny, or in any warm part of the house. The pickle should be shaken regularly for several weeks until the skins have softened and lemons have lost their bitterness; it should then be left to steep for at least 6 months before being used.

The jar of pickled lemons we made quite recently has become a familiar piece of furniture in our sitting-room. It has its place alongside an old marble clock on the mantelpiece above the fire, and 'shaking the pickle' has now become as natural as winding the clock. Both operations are done regularly by anyone who happens to be standing by the mantelpiece.

A similar pickle can be made by using limes instead of lemons. This may be more expensive unless you live in a town with West Indian or Asian shops and vegetable stalls, where limes are often cheaper than lemons. Limes soften much more quickly than lemons, and should be ready within a week, so you must keep a careful check on how they are progressing. Use about half the quantity of salt with limes, or their flavour will become overpowering. But otherwise the recipe is exactly the same as for lemons.

Both pickled limes and pickled lemons are very good with a great variety of hot, highly spiced dishes like curries, couscous and pilaffs, particularly when there is rice or some other ingredient to absorb the excess vinegar and citrus juice. These pickles are less successful with cold meats.

Pickled Radish Pods

Radishes are one of the easiest vegetables to grow, whatever the size of your garden. The first sowings can be made in March or April, the seeds being sown in $\frac{1}{2}$ inch drills. The important thing to remember is that radishes must have a fast growing season; the seedlings should be thinned early, and the crop picked young. Radishes which have been left in the ground too long rapidly turn woody and spongy inside; this is particularly true with the first sowings, when the weather is most unpredictable. But if these unusable radishes are left in the ground, allowed to flower and eventually to go to seed, the odd-looking green pods can be successfully pickled. Radish pods were valued as a vegetable for inclusion in mixed pickle and piccalilli by nineteenth-century writers such as Mrs Beeton and Eliza Acton, but they seem to have completely disappeared from today's cookery books – which is a great pity since they have a striking pungent taste, not at all that of a cultivated vegetable.

The pods should be picked before they become too large. They should be put at once in hot brine and left there until the brine is cold. If they are now bright green they are ready for pickling. If not, the brine should be boiled up once more and poured over the pods and the process repeated until they look green. Then wash the pods free of salt, drain and pack into jars with a few small red chilli peppers. These will give the pickle colour as well as flavour. Cover the pods with white vinegar which has been boiled and allowed to cool. Seal and store until the winter. Pickled radish pods are a useful substitute for chives, and can be used like them in potato salad or chopped and mixed with cream cheese.

Indian Mixed Pickle

a variety of vegetables and fruit, e.g. a white cabbage, cauliflower, French beans, cucumbers, small onions, nasturtium seeds, radish pods, melon, plums, apples, red and green peppers; white vinegar; for each quart allow: 2 cloves garlic; 1 oz. bruised root ginger; $\frac{1}{2}$ oz. black peppercorns; 4 cloves; 1 tsp. whole allspice; $\frac{1}{2}$ tsp. cayenne pepper; $\frac{1}{2}$ oz. mustard seed; 1 tsp. turmeric.

The main point about this pickle is that it can be started early in the summer and kept going as various fruits and vegetables come into season. If you use fruit in the pickle, it must be green.

Cut the cabbage, which should be hard and white, into slices, and the cauliflower into small branches. Sprinkle salt over them and leave for 24 hours. Next day wash and dry them and put them in the largest jar that you can find. Add the chopped garlic, allspice, peppercorns, bruised ginger and cloves. Boil up sufficient white vinegar to cover the vegetables, pour it hot over them, and cover the jar when cold.

From then on, as vegetables and fruit come into season, they can be added to the jar. Remember that they must be salted in the same way as the cabbage and cauliflower before being put in the vinegar, and make sure that when they are added they are covered by the vinegar. If not, some vinegar will have to be boiled up and poured over them. When you have all the vegetables you require, turn them out into a large pan and mix well. Then put the vegetables without the vinegar into small jars. Boil up the vinegar with the other spices (turmeric, mustard seed, and cayenne pepper), pour the hot vinegar over the vegetables, and cover well. This pickle is best made as a large batch for use throughout the year and if the vegetables are well covered it will last for a long time.

Pickled Walnuts

The jar of pickled walnuts occupied a special place at home when I was a small boy. It was eaten on one occasion only – Boxing Day lunchtime, with cold chicken and ham. My mother would buy the jar some weeks before Christmas, and store it away in the highest cupboard in the kitchen. Since then I've always had a particular affection for this pickle; in fact it's the only manufactured pickle that I now enjoy.

Unfortunately there has been a steady decline in the number of walnut trees growing in this country since the eighteenth century, mainly due to the popularity of walnut wood for furniture. Those trees that are left bear little or no fruit, so unless you know of a source of young walnuts, you will have to be content with the ready-made pickle. But there was a time when walnuts were plentiful, and young lads would go out 'walnut dashing' – that is, beating the young nuts off the trees with long sticks. However, if you do locate a source of walnuts, they should be picked in June or July, when they are still green, and before they harden.

Pickled walnuts became particularly popular in Victorian London. In gentlemen's clubs they were the favourite accompaniment to mutton chops grilled on a gridiron, and in pubs they were served with cold roast beef in sandwiches, and with Stilton cheese and brown bread. They were also put into casseroles, and steak and kidney puddings, often as a substitute for oysters. My own favourite is walnuts and cold chicken.

(1) Pick the walnuts when they are still green, before the shells have begun to form. (The first part of the shell appears opposite the stalk about $\frac{1}{4}$ inch from the end.) Prick the nuts with a needle. Make up a brine using 2 oz. salt per pint of water and soak the nuts in this for several days. Then change the water and soak for a further week. Drain well and spread out the nuts onto dishes so that they quickly turn black. You may need to turn them so that their whole surface is exposed.

When they are completely black, put them carefully into jars and cover with spiced vinegar. This is made up as follows:

1 pint malt vinegar; 2 tsp. freshly grated horseradish; 1 tsp. whole allspice; 1 tsp. black peppercorns.

Boil the ingredients together for 10 minutes, then strain and pour the vinegar hot over the walnuts. Cover well and keep for a month before using.

(2) This nineteenth-century recipe is one of the most interesting for pickling walnuts, even if it may seem a little impractical nowadays:

Get a hundred of fine large walnuts while the shells are yet tender, wrap them up in vine leaves separately, put them into jars along with plenty more vine leaves, so that they cannot suffer by contact with each other, and cover with the best light coloured vinegar. Make secure from the air and let them remain so for three weeks. Now pour off the vinegar, wrap up again the fruit in fresh vine leaves and fill the jars with vinegar as before. This must be continued two weeks longer when you may take off the leaves, put the fruit into jars, and make the following pickle for them: –
3 qts of pale vinegar with enough salt in it to float an egg; 1½ oz. garlic minced; 2 oz. ground cloves; 1 oz. ground mace; 1½ oz. ground allspice; 2 oz. ground nutmeg.
Let these simmer 15 minutes and pour the whole boiling hot over the walnuts. Keep four months before breaking in on them.
> *The Art & Mystery of Curing, Preserving and Potting,*
> by A Wholesale Curer of Comestibles, Chapman &
> Hall, 1864

If you manage to get some walnuts you will probably need to scale down the quantities in this recipe. The vine leaves can be omitted without any great damage being done to the nuts, although they do add an interesting flavour, and help in preserving the pickle.

Pickled Asparagus

When asparagus was pickled in the eighteenth century, cooks thought nothing of using 200 sticks at a time; nowadays the crop is scarce – it's costly in the shops and treasured fresh if it is grown in the garden. But for a little extravagance, some sticks pickled in wine vinegar are excellent. The whole process is one of careful handling and a sensitive blending of flavours – no rough and ready techniques or overpowering tastes.

asparagus (as many sticks as you can spare); a pickle made of: $\frac{1}{4}$ tsp. white pepper; $\frac{1}{2}$ tsp. freshly grated nutmeg; 3 blades of mace; 1 pint wine vinegar (or $\frac{1}{2}$ pint dry white wine and $\frac{1}{2}$ pint wine vinegar).

Choose sticks of asparagus that are full grown, fat and straight. Cut off the base ends leaving only the tender green parts of the stick (so that they are no longer than about 5 inches). Wash them carefully in cold water, and leave them in a bowl of slightly salted water for a couple of hours. While the asparagus is soaking, make up a pickle with the vinegar and spices and boil it for about 10 minutes. Then put the sticks into a saucepan with just enough water to cover them. Don't overload the saucepan – if necessary, do this part of the operation in several stages so that the asparagus is not damaged. Bring to the boil and immediately remove the pan from the heat and carefully take out the sticks of asparagus. Lay them on a cloth to drain and get cold, then stack them carefully upright into jars and pour over the cold spiced vinegar. Cover and seal in the usual way. It is not advisable to keep this pickle for a long time; use it a week or two after it has been made. The asparagus is a good addition to imaginative salads, and it also goes well with the delicate flavour and texture of cold smoked or fresh fish, and marinaded herrings.

Marrow Mangoes

One of the prized discoveries of the traders of the East India Company was the mango, and from about 1700 onwards cooks and housewives devised ingenious methods of imitating the taste and texture of this fruit using melons, cucumbers, lemons, peaches and vegetable marrows. These 'mangoes', as they were called, were an elaborate kind of pickle in which the fruit or vegetable was hollowed out and filled with various spiced ingredients. Whilst the resemblance to real mangoes is debatable, these pickles are still among the most interesting that you can make.

All the recipes are similar, but our real favourite is the marrow mango. You can of course use one of the other vegetables and adapt the recipe to your own needs.

The first time that we made this pickle we didn't use a true marrow, but an oversize courgette that we had neglected to pick from our garden when it was small. It had grown unnoticed and weighed nearly three pounds.

a small vegetable marrow (2–3 lb. is a convenient size); malt vinegar; sugar (4 oz. per pint of vinegar); 2 chopped onions; 1 tsp. grated horseradish; 2 tsp. mustard seed; 4 pieces root ginger; 10 black peppercorns.

Peel the marrow, cut it in half lengthways and scoop out the seeds. Then put it to soak overnight in salt water. Next day prepare the filling. (It's difficult to give exact quantities here, as so much depends on the shape and size of the marrow, how much you have hollowed out and how fiery you want your pickle to be. But the mixture given above should be a useful guide.) When you have the mixture ready, drain the marrow and pack the seed space with the filling. Tie the halves together with string. You will probably need to secure the marrow with about 3 pieces of string along its length otherwise too much of the filling will escape. Then put the marrow into a large stone jar or pot and cover it with a boiling solution of vinegar. Put a cloth over the jar to keep out flies. Next day drain off the vinegar and re-boil. This should be repeated every day until the marrow looks dark and soft (it takes about 10 days). Don't worry if a little of the mixture does escape during handling and steeping; in fact this is useful as it spices the vinegar. When the marrow is ready, take it out of the vinegar, open it up and remove the filling. Slice the marrow into good pieces and pack in jars. Then boil up the vinegar with some sugar (4 oz. per pint) and pour it hot over the marrow pieces. Cover well and store in a cool, dry place.

Marrow mangoes should be stored at least 3 months before being opened. The interesting thing about this pickle is the variation in taste of different pieces. Some have an overpowering hot taste, whilst others are milder, with just a hint of onion flavour. But it's quite random, depending on the way the spices have been placed inside the marrow. This gives the pickle an element of surprise: a friend of ours, enjoying our pickles one evening, decided to consume a piece of marrow mango whole. He delved into the jar with his hand and removed one of the largest pieces which he thrust confidently into his mouth. A few seconds later he was red-faced and sweating, but bearing his agonies in silence. We knew then that he had chosen the wrong piece and that he would suffer drastic after-effects.

Pickled Elder Buds

This pickle seems to have been quite popular in the eighteenth century, and there are a surprising number of references to it in recipe books and writings of the period. Apparently it was considered to be a worthy imitation of bamboo shoots – one of the delicacies brought back by the seamen of the East India Company.

Put the buds into vinegar, seasoned with salt, whole pepper, large mace, lemon peel cut small, let them have two or three warms over the fire; then take them out, and let the buds and the pickle both cool, then put the buds into your pot, and cover them with the pickle.

This recipe comes from *The Receipt Book of John Mott, Cook to the Duke of Bolton* (1723). Another eighteenth-century recipe uses 'allegar' – vinegar made from sour ale and contains the following directions:

put [the buds] into a brass pan, cover them with vine leaves and pour the water on them that they come out of; set them over a slow fire till they are quite green.

This is one more example of the dangerous use of brass to produce a threatening green colour in pickles.

Another unlikely imitation, similar to 'mangoes' and pickled elder buds was 'mock ginger', which was made from peeled cauliflower stalks with large quantities of turmeric and other spices in wine vinegar.

Pickled Nasturtium Seeds

nasturtium seeds; bay leaves; peppercorns; salt; white vinegar.

If you grow nasturtiums then it's worth making full use of them as a food. The pickled seeds are a substitute for the more expensive capers; they can be made into a sauce for fish or added to salads, where their strange hot taste will give a boost to those indifferent concoctions of

lettuce and cucumber. The flowers are useful too, not only for decoration, but also for flavouring a sauce (see Nasturtium Sauce, p. 117).

Pick the nasturtium seeds on a hot dry day, soon after the blossom has left the plant, and wash them well, making sure you get rid of any insect life that might be lurking in the wrinkles. Drain them, and put into a dish in a cool oven to dry.

Meanwhile, put the vinegar into a saucepan with a teaspoon of salt per pint, a couple of bay leaves and a few peppercorns. Boil and allow to cool. When the nasturtium seeds have dried pack them into jars with the bay leaves and peppercorns, pour over the cold vinegar, and cover.

The seeds should be left to pickle for at least 3 months before being used.

Pickled Ash Keys

The young, green fruits of the ash should be picked in June or July for pickling, before they become too tough and bitter. Boil the keys until they are soft, discard the water if it tastes bitter, and re-boil with fresh water. Then drain the keys and cover with white vinegar which has also been boiled. Cover and store for some weeks before using.

Pickled Cucumbers

(1) *Dill Pickles*

cucumbers; fennel stalks and seeds; dill seeds; coriander seeds; black peppercorns; salt; white vinegar.

The cucumber is a vegetable with a bad reputation; we think of it as indigestible, tasteless and lacking in versatility – qualities which derive from the vegetable's customary role in the unimaginative English salad. But it is not without its uses – particularly fried and as a pickle. The use of fennel and dill was a stroke of near genius by those cooks who, in the seventeenth century, first pickled cucumbers in this way.

Choose cucumbers which are young, fresh and rather small. These will be very crisp and, equally important, they will have few pips. The fennel, dill and coriander seeds can be bought from most delicatessens. If you can pick some fresh fennel stalks from the plant that grows along many roadsides this is best; if not use more dill seeds in your pickle, or purchase some dill weed (dried and powdered dill leaves) which will be a good substitute. When you have gathered all the ingredients together, chop the cucumber unpeeled into slices about $\frac{1}{4}$ inch thick and put into a bowl of salt and water (2 oz. per pint) for about 2 hours, making sure the cucumber is completely immersed. Then drain and rinse well. If you have some fennel stalks, wash them and chop them roughly into 1 inch lengths. Take time here to enjoy the smell of chopped fennel: when cut it releases tingling fumes like aniseed, which have the same exhilarating effect as early morning air at the seaside.

You can now begin to fill some clean, dry, wide-mouthed jars with the various ingredients. Put some chopped fennel at the bottom of the jar, and then a layer of cucumber. Continue to fill up the jar in layers, as you please, tossing in a few seeds where they seem appropriate. When the jar is full boil up the vinegar and salt in a saucepan (about 2 tsp. to each pint of vinegar); allow it to cool, pour it over the cucumber, then cover. This pickle will be ready for use after a month or so, but keeps well and is good for 2 to 3 months.

These dill pickles have a number of uses. As well as being eaten with cold meat and fish, they can be chopped and put into hors d'oeuvres, salad dressings and in dishes like that refreshing cold soup, okroshka.

(2) This is a method for pickling cucumbers whole that resembles the process used for making 'mangoes'. You will need a large, tall glass jar such as a sweet jar for this.

whole cucumbers; salt; a mixture containing grated horseradish, shallots, capers, nutmeg, mustard seed and sugar; white vinegar.

Choose cucumbers that are fat and straight if possible. Cut a triangular wedge from each one using a very sharp knife. This wedge should run the whole length of the cucumber and should be a manageable size. Put the cucumbers and wedges into a shallow dish and scatter with salt. Leave overnight. Next day wash them free of salt and drain well. Then make up a mixture of the spices. You can alter the amounts of the various ingredients to suit your own taste and the quantity of pickle you are making, but the following mixture is a useful guide:

2 shallots; 2 tsp. grated horseradish; 1 tsp. capers; 1 tsp. sugar; 2 tsp. mustard seed; $\frac{1}{2}$ tsp. grated nutmeg.

77

Chop the shallots and capers finely and mix all the ingredients together. Fill the cucumbers with this, replace the wedges and secure in place with fine string. You will need to tie several pieces along the length of each cucumber. Pack the cucumbers upright in the jar and cover with white vinegar that has been boiled and allowed to cool. Seal and store the jars in a dry place for a month before using.

The best way to use these cucumbers is to cut off slices or chunks as you need them; cut a piece from a cucumber and then replace the remainder in the pickle.

Pickled Aubergines

This recipe is something of an oddity. The combination of aubergines and carrots is outside the tradition of English pickle making; this particular recipe probably derives from Bulgarian cookery. It includes the suggestion that strands from the outside of celery should be used as a kind of edible string.

aubergines; chopped carrots and garlic; wine vinegar; strands from celery stalks.

Choose good quality aubergines, preferably large and round, rather than long and thin. Cut them lengthwise in half and scoop out the core of spongy flesh. Put the halves into salted water and boil for 2 minutes. Drain the aubergines and stuff them with a mixture of chopped carrots and garlic. Put the halves together and secure with strands from the outside of celery stalks. Put the aubergines carefully into a wide-mouthed glass jar and cover with hot wine vinegar. Cover and store for a couple of weeks before using. This pickle should be used quickly, as it does not keep well.

Pickled Samphire

Marsh samphire, or glasswort (*Salicornia europaea*) is a plant very well known to East Anglians, and is common on saltmarshes round most British coasts. But whilst it is eaten and appreciated where it does grow, it's a vegetable that you'll rarely find in restaurants or shops, although a few places like the fish stalls on Norwich market do sell it. In most cases you will see it in company with cod and cockles in the fishmonger's, rather than with 'land vegetables' in the greengrocer's. We only discovered the real joys of samphire by actually picking it ourselves.

We would go out at low tide during the hot days of July and August, when the samphire is at its best, armed with scissors, a sharp fish-gutting knife and an onion net. Finding the samphire wasn't difficult. After plunging through boggy marshes and across muddy creeks, like over-confident explorers, we would see the plant nestling along the sheltered edges of gulleys and creeks, or else sprawling across acres of flat ground like a badly kept lawn. We picked the samphire by snipping it off at the base with scissors or, sometimes, by pulling it up and using the knife to cut off the roots. Before leaving the marshes we packed the samphire into the onion net and waded out into the middle of a creek to wash the harvest. We then headed homeward, with aching backs and sore thumbs, our faces reddened by the east wind.

The lure of samphire was so strong that I can recall on one occasion I had decided to walk out onto the marshes around Blakeney on the North Norfolk coast without Rose, and I stumbled onto a vast patch of samphire. As I had not come prepared for picking yet was unable to ignore this inviting forest, I proceeded to get as much as I could, and to use my boots and socks as containers. When these were crammed full of samphire I waded barefoot towards dry land, the crop bulging out of my footwear. I must indeed have been a strange spectacle, as I made my way from the quay, up the hill to the pub.

In Blakeney I was told about the old way of pickling samphire. It was packed into jars with vinegar and put in the ovens of the local bakery on a Friday night when they were cooling off, and left there until the following Monday morning. It's difficult to imagine what condition the samphire was in after this treatment, but it seems to have been greatly valued. A less drastic and slightly more practical recipe is this one:

1 pint samphire; 1 oz. salt; $\frac{1}{2}$ oz. grated horseradish; $\frac{1}{2}$ oz. black peppercorns; 1 pint cider vinegar.

When you have picked the samphire wash and drain it well. Then pack it into a jar with the horseradish and peppercorns. (You can use horseradish you have dug and grated yourself.) Boil the cider vinegar with the salt for 10 minutes, and pour hot over the samphire. Then cover the jar and put it in a warm oven for 1 hour.

The main problem with pickling samphire is to find a way to keep the samphire itself reasonably crisp. We had worked out a method of keeping the samphire in very strong brine, and it was encouraging to see a similar method suggested by Hannah Glasse. In theory this should work although we have not yet tried it. Store the samphire in brine and when you want to use it, take it out, wash and steep in vinegar for an hour or so before eating.

Although samphire, boiled and saturated with melted butter, goes well with roast meat, particularly lamb, we prefer it with a freshly caught dab fried in butter. The pairing of samphire and lamb stems from the traditional way of complementing meat and vegetables; the animal was eaten with the food on which it lived. So sheep which grazed on marsh samphire were eaten with it. When samphire is pickled it can be eaten with cold lamb, or with a dish of cockles steeped in vinegar and pepper and served with brown bread.

A similar pickle can be made using rock samphire (*Crithmum maritimum*), a plant that likes rocky coasts and shingle beaches. In fact this was the species first made into a pickle and there is a recipe for it in John Evelyn's *Acetaria* of 1699.

Perhaps the most intriguing use of pickled rock samphire was in Star-Gazey Pie. This was a strangely designed fish pie that made use of whole pilchards. The name referred not only to the geometric star-like arrangement of the fish, like spokes in a wheel, but also to the fact that the fish heads poked out of the pie and gave the impression of literally gazing starwards. There were good reasons for this construction; the fish heads were left on even though the fish were boned because they contained oil that was allowed to drain back into the pie; and they were not covered with pastry because that was thought to be wasteful. Inside the pie, the fish were stuffed with various mixtures including pickled samphire.

Pickled Pears
small firm pears; white vinegar; for each pint use: ½ lb. white sugar; 6 cloves; rind of ½ lemon; 1 small stick of cinnamon; 4 pieces root ginger.

Choose small pears that are not at all mushy; the variety 'Conference' is very suitable. Peel and core them and cut into quarters lengthways. Keep the fruit in a bowl of water while you are preparing the pickle; this prevents discoloration. Put the cloves, lemon peel, cinnamon stick and root ginger into a muslin bag and boil in the vinegar for about 10 minutes. Remove the bag and add the sugar, stirring until it is dissolved. Then add the pears and simmer in the pickle until they are just tender. Remove the fruit carefully and pack into warm jars. Bring the syrupy vinegar to the boil and pour hot over the fruit. Make sure that it is well covered since some of the liquid tends to be absorbed by the fruit during storage. Cover and store for three months before use. This recipe can be used for apples and quinces.

Pickled Blackberries
2½ lb. blackberries; 1 lb. sugar; ½ pint white wine vinegar; 2 leaves rose geranium.

Put the sugar into a pan with the wine vinegar and simmer until it is dissolved. Then add the blackberries. These should be the largest and sweetest you can find and not too ripe (the first fruit to ripen at the very tip of a bramble are the best). Simmer for 5 minutes or so, just long enough to soften the fruit without making them disintegrate. Then carefully remove the fruit and transfer to jars. Boil up the vinegar and sugar until a thick syrup is formed. Put the geranium leaves in with the fruit and pour over the syrup while still hot. Cover and store for a week or so before using.

These spiced fruit, slightly sharp and perfumed with geranium, are the perfect accompaniment to soft French cream cheeses. This is food for the last days of summer before fires have to be lit and curtains drawn against damp autumn evenings.

Keep the syrupy vinegar that is left after all the blackberries have been eaten.

Pickled Redcurrants

Redcurrants are delicate and delectable. This recipe makes use of both bunches and single berries, which play different roles in the preparation of the pickle. The imagination and good sense behind this recipe ensure that the process matches the qualities of the fruit. If you want to make this pickle, however, you will need to pick the redcurrants yourself; only that way can you ensure that you have a good mixture of bunches and single fruit.

Take currants for this purpose just before they have attained a perfect red colour. Select the nicest bunches and keep these separate. Accept no single ones unless they are clear and sound. Boil the single fruit in the following mixture until a good colour is obtained:

white sugar ½ lb.; salt 2 oz.; bay leaves a few; white wine or vinegar 1 pt.

Skim it well and let it get cold. Then strain it nicely and press the fruit through a sieve to obtain as much of the colour as possible. Boil again and skim till quite clear. Now place the bunches into glass jars and pour the hot liquor over them so that they are completely immersed. Then cover.

Adapted from *The Art & Mystery of Curing, Potting and Preserving*, by A Wholesale Curer of Comestibles, Chapman & Hall, 1864

If the bunches have been carefully placed in the jars, they can be removed intact, and eaten like miniature bunches of grapes.

Pickled Cherries
2 lb. ripe red cherries; 1 pint white wine vinegar; 2 tsp. coriander seeds; 2 blades mace; 1 tsp. black peppercorns.

Choose cherries that are sound and not over-ripe. Wash and drain them and leave about 1 inch of stalk on each one; this makes eating much easier. Put the cherries in a jar and cover with cold white wine vinegar. Allow to stand for a week. Then drain off the vinegar and add to it the spices tied in a muslin bag. Boil for 10 minutes. Allow the pickle to go cold and pour it over the cherries packed in jars. Cover and store for a month before using.

The vinegar from this pickle makes a good syrup if a pound of sugar is added to each pint of liquid and boiled up. If a few raspberries or currants are infused in the vinegar for several days the syrup is much improved.

If you have black cherries, a sweet pickle might be more suitable. Make a syrup of the following:

1 pint white wine vinegar; 8 oz. brown sugar; 2 large sticks cinnamon; 1 tsp. cloves.

Put the spices in a muslin bag and add to the vinegar and sugar in a pan. Boil for 10 minutes. Add the cherries and simmer for a further 15 minutes. Then remove the cherries and pack into jars. Boil up the liquid once more until it has a good syrupy consistency, then pour hot over the cherries. Cover and store. This is a rich preserve that demands luxurious accompaniments.

Pickled Damsons
We had gone out looking for crabapples. It was an evening in the first week of September, and before the sun had completely vanished below the outline of the surrounding heath, I sensed that autumn had come; it had, quite suddenly, turned cold. We were at the end of a lane on a dwindling summer's evening and the climate was deceiving us – for

83

the twilight and misty air had no place in this season. They belonged with the early mornings of winter.

Rose travelled ahead on the moped whilst I followed precariously in her wake on a bicycle without lights. As we searched the hedgerows we found some crabapple trees, misshapen with age, and beyond saw unfamiliar bluish fruit among some even more aged branches. We were lucky. The light was fading and the fruit might have gone unnoticed, but having spotted one, and recognized it as a damson, we searched harder, eventually collecting sufficient for our use. There was a time not too long ago when damsons were nearly as common as blackberries. Like crabapples they were planted in orchards and along the edges of farmland. But age, over-picking and ill-treatment have all but finished them. As it was, we picked about a pound of fruit from half a dozen 'ancient damson trees'.

1 lb. damsons; 8 oz. sugar; 2 pieces stick cinnamon; 6 cloves; 4 pieces of root ginger; malt vinegar.

Wash and clean the damsons, removing their stalks. Then put the fruit into an earthenware dish and sprinkle with the sugar. Pour on enough malt vinegar to cover the damsons and, after adding the spices, put the dish at the bottom of a warm oven to cook very slowly. This is important since the damsons must remain intact; if cooked too quickly the skins will split. After about 20 minutes, when the damsons begin to feel soft, and the juice is running, take out the dish and allow it to cool. When cold strain the juice, boil it in a saucepan and pour it over the fruit. This straining and boiling should be repeated every day for 10 days, then the damsons should be left in the juice for another week. By this time they are wrinkled and their skins are hard; the juice is syrupy and the colour of well-kept port. Strain the damsons and pack them into a jar; boil up the juice once more and pour it hot over them. Seal the jar.

Pickled damsons can be kept for a long time – in fact age improves them. But the first jar that I made was eaten quite young with cold pheasant and rowan jelly. It was a surprising, but effective combination – the bitter, smoky flavour of the rowan offset by the slightly sharp taste of our damsons.

Pickled Plums

2 lb. plums; 1 lb. demerara sugar; cloves; a good piece of stick cinnamon; malt vinegar.

Choose plums that are slightly under-ripe, and prick them with a needle. (This will help to keep the plums intact and prevent their skins from splitting when they are cooked.) Stick a clove into one end of each plum. Arrange the plums in a fireproof dish with the sugar, cinnamon and sufficient vinegar to cover them. Put the dish (with a lid on) into a warm oven (250°F) for about 30 minutes or until the plums begin to feel soft. Remove the dish and allow it to stand until the next day. Then strain the fruit and carefully pack them into jars. Boil up the juice and simmer for 30 minutes. We find it best to add a little more sugar at this stage to give the juice a thicker consistency. Pour the hot liquid over the fruit and cover when cold.

Keep the pickled plums at least 3 months before using them. By this time the skins have hardened and wrinkled, but the flesh of the fruit is still soft and spicy. We eat these plums with roast meat and chicken, and they're superb with cold pork pie. (Remember that there is a clove in the end of each plum before biting into it.)

Pickled Prunes

2 lb. large prunes; 8 oz. sugar; pinch nutmeg; pinch mace; 1 tsp. black pepper; 1 pint malt vinegar.

First soak the prunes in cold water for about 10 hours until they are plump and juicy. When they are ready drain them well and pack into jars. Boil the vinegar, sugar and spices together for about 10 minutes and pour hot over the prunes, making sure they are completely covered. If you have an open bottle of brandy in the house, a tablespoon added to this pickle considerably improves its flavour.

Although the prunes can be used shortly after bottling, we have found that they are much better if left for several months before opening. They are spicy and slightly sharp tasting and go very well with cold ham.

Pickled Eggs

These became common in England at the beginning of the eighteenth century and a large jar of them was a familiar sight in most farmhouses, particularly around Eastertime when the farm chickens were at their best. Of course nowadays fewer people have a free supply of eggs, so pickling is only really worthwhile if you can obtain cheap produce. Luckily we get trays of eggs from a local farmer, often as payment for helping him with his milk round.

We always leave our eggs a few days before attempting to pickle them, since very fresh eggs are difficult to shell after being boiled – the white tends to adhere to the shell itself, and you are left with an object more like an ill-fated, uncooked meringue. The essence of egg pickling is to use plain malt vinegar and to be patient enough to let this permeate the eggs. The outside should be brown, like a new shell, whilst the yolk is soft and creamy.

You will need a large, wide-mouthed jar for this pickle. First boil some eggs for 10–15 minutes. At the same time, boil some plain malt vinegar in another saucepan. When the eggs are cooked, put them into cold water to cool and then shell them (we always use the handle of a teaspoon for this). Put into the jar and cover with the hot vinegar. You can always add more eggs when you have them to spare. They will be ready after 2–3 weeks, but improve with longer keeping.

Pickled eggs can be eaten as an accompaniment to cold meat or cheese, but they are at their best with beer. Thankfully there are still a few pubs in Suffolk that make their own pickled eggs, and our favourite recollections of them are as a part of long evenings with darts and pints of locally brewed mild.

Incidentally, they have given rise to a new type of snack, in which they are eaten with potato crisps – an egg rests uncomfortably inside the open packet on a bed of brown crispy fragments. It's a curious amalgam of the traditional pickle with today's convenience food, but it works. The effect is tasty *and* functional since the crisps tend to absorb any excess vinegar from the egg.

FLAVOURED VINEGARS

These are very useful additions to the larder, as pleasant alternatives to plain vinegar or as reviving drinks. There are several distinct types, the most common being herb and fruit vinegars. Herb vinegars are simply made by steeping some of the herb – marjoram, tarragon, mint, basil etc., in the vinegar for a certain length of time until it is well flavoured. The resulting vinegar can be used in making pickles, or in salad dressings and sauces.

Fruit vinegars are slightly different. Made from raspberries, black-currants or blackberries they are renowned as cordials, either hot for the relief of sore throats, or ice-cold to restore one's stamina on a hot summer's day. After the fruit has steeped in vinegar, the strained liquid is sweetened with sugar or honey.

As well as these flavoured vinegars, there are a number of home-brewed vinegars which can be made. Around the turn of the century, when manufactured vinegar was quite often of dubious quality, country people made their own vinegars from cowslips, primroses, gooseberries and rhubarb. These were like partially fermented wines which were allowed to mature at least a year in barrels and bottles. There are also methods of turning home-made fruit wines into vinegars.

Remember that the vinegar left over from many pickles can be used on its own – it doesn't have to be thrown away. For example, the vinegar from pickled onions and pickled walnuts can be used in certain ketchups, and celery and cucumber vinegars are very good for salad dressings. There is plenty of room for experiment here; you can use a variety of herbs and combinations of flavours and you can even blend vinegars together like wines.

Tarragon Vinegar

First of all it is important to make a distinction between French tarragon (*Artemisia dracunculus*), and its inferior relative Russian or False tarragon (*Artemisia dracunculoides*). The latter can be grown easily from seed, but its flavour cannot match that of the true French variety. This needs a warm dry climate and is usually only propagated from cuttings or root division. You should use French tarragon for making vinegar.

Gather tarragon just before it blossoms, usually around the end of July, and strip the leaves from the larger stalks. Pack the herb into a glass jar and cover with white wine vinegar. If you have fresh tarragon use about 2 oz. to every pint of vinegar; with dried tarragon put in 1 tablespoon per pint. For this preparation it's really essential that you use white wine vinegar – don't try to save money by substituting distilled vinegar as this completely alters the subtle flavour created by the wine and herb. Let the tarragon steep for at least a month, then strain it into a new bottle, and add a fresh branch of tarragon; this improves the flavour of the vinegar considerably.

Tarragon vinegar is really the most versatile of all the herb vinegars. It can be used when making Tartare sauce, Béarnaise sauce and it is a good dressing for tomatoes and with fish and chicken salads.

Similar vinegars can be made using other herbs, such as sage, thyme, marjoram, mint or basil. The recipe is the same in each case, except that the basil vinegar is ready in a couple of weeks.

Horseradish Vinegar

This is best made with freshly grated horseradish, so first of all you will need to find and dig up a good root. When you have peeled and shredded the horseradish put it into a jar with a chopped onion, and top up with hot malt vinegar. (The quantity of horseradish used can vary, but if you reckon to half-fill the jar with it, this will give you a very strongly flavoured vinegar.) When the jar has cooled, cover and give it a good shake, and let it stand for several weeks in a warm place, shaking occasionally. After about 6 weeks, taste the vinegar; if it is sufficiently flavoured for your own taste, then it can be strained and re-bottled, and is ready for use. If not, let it stand for a few weeks more.

In his *Herball* of 1597, John Gerard says: 'The horseradish, stamped with a little vinegar put thereto, is commonly used for sauce to eate fish with and such like meates as we do mustarde.' The comparison with mustard is a valuable one, and gives a good indication of the uses of horseradish vinegar; it is best when used against oily fish and fatty meat. Try it on fish and chips instead of plain malt vinegar.

You can make similar vinegars using chopped shallots or sliced garlic. The strength of these vinegars is really a matter of personal taste, but a useful guide is 3 cloves of garlic or 4 shallots per pint of vinegar.

Elderflower Vinegar

Go out at the end of June, when the elderflowers are in full bloom, and pick some bunches. When you get home strip the flowers from the stalks by gently rolling the flowers between finger and thumb. Make sure there are no insects lurking among the frothy clusters. Half-fill a jar with the flowers, well packed down, and top up with white wine vinegar. Leave in a warm place or 'under the influence of sunbeams' for 2 weeks, before testing the vinegar. If the flavour is right, then strain through a jelly bag and bottle. It should be well sealed and stored in a dry place.

Elderberry Vinegar

1 pint white vinegar; 12 oz. elderberries; 12 oz. white sugar.

Put the elderberries and vinegar together in a jar, cover and leave for several days. Shake the contents occasionally. Strain off the vinegar through a sieve, put it into a saucepan and add the required amount of sugar, stirring until dissolved. Then bring it to the boil, allow the vinegar to cool, bottle and store in the usual way.

Blackberry Vinegar

1 pint ripe blackberries; 1 pint white wine vinegar; 1 lb. white sugar; 8 oz. thin honey.

This is a good way of making use of very ripe fruit. Put the blackberries and the vinegar into a jar with a good cover and leave them to steep for a week or so, giving them a shake quite frequently. Then strain through a sieve and put into a saucepan. Add the sugar and the honey, stirring until they are dissolved. Bring to the boil slowly. Allow the vinegar to cool, transfer it to bottles and seal well. The vinegar should be stored in a dry, dark cupboard.

Raspberry Vinegar

Here is a pleasant 'refresher', specially suitable for the young after lawn tennis or sports on hot days, but acceptable also to their elders when exhausted by church, depressed by gardening, or exasperated by shopping.

Take one pound of raspberries to every pint best white vinegar. Let it stand for a fortnight in a covered jar in a cool larder. Then strain without pressure, and to every pint add 12 ounces white sugar. Boil ten minutes, let cool and bottle in nice medium-sized bottles saved perhaps from some present of foreign liqueurs.

A teaspoonful stirred into a tumbler of water with a lump of ice, or introduced to a very cold syphon will taste like the elixir of life on a hot day, and is pretty as it is pleasant.

Kitchen Essays, Lady Jekyll, Collins, 1968

This is perfect. We have included it in full because if ever a recipe reflected a whole social landscape it is this one. Unquestionably it belongs to the English aristocracy of the 1920s.

Blackcurrant Vinegar

3 lb. blackcurrants; 1 quart white vinegar; white sugar.

Wash the blackcurrants and remove any pieces of leaf or stalk. Bruise about half of them with a wooden spoon, and cover with the vinegar. Leave for 24 hours in a bowl. Decant the juice and pour it over the rest of the bruised currants. Leave for another 24 hours, then strain the whole through a jelly bag, allowing the juice to drip of its own accord. (Squeezing the bag to speed up the process will make the vinegar cloudy.) Measure the volume of the juice, and for each pint add 1 lb. of sugar. Heat gently in a preserving pan for about 10 minutes, stirring until the sugar is dissolved. Allow the vinegar to cool, bottle it, seal securely and store in a dark dry cupboard.

Primrose Vinegar

At the end of the last century commercially sold vinegar tended to be of dubious quality because of adulteration, so when facilities were available vinegar was often made in the home. In the country these vinegars were based on fruit and flowers, and primrose was the most highly valued. The technique had much in common with the method of making plain vinegar in the eighteenth century, except that the basic flavour was altered by using primroses, gooseberries or rhubarb.

The ingredients for primrose vinegar in this recipe are characteristically excessive, but I have chosen to retain them, to give a sense of the scale of home production in those days.

cold water 30 quarts; brown sugar 12 lb; primroses a peck; compressed yeast 1 or 2 ounces.

Boil the water and the sugar together for 10 minutes. When it is cold add a peck of primrose petals and the yeast creamed with a little sugar. Let it work a few days, stirring it often. Then put it in a barrel with the primroses. Keep it close and near the fire. It must stand a year.

> Recipe included in *Good Things in England,*
> compiled and edited by Florence White,
> Jonathan Cape, 1932

Home-Brewed Vinegars

If you make home-made wines and are used to the processes of home-brewing, then you will not find these vinegars too difficult. You will need either cider or a mixture of equal quantities of wine and water as your starting material. This is a good way of using wine that has gone sour, and would otherwise be condemned to the drain.

Unlike wine making, vinegar making needs air to oxidize the alcohol to acetic acid, so you will notice the directions say that the brewing container should only be *half-full.*

To every five parts of cider or diluted wine add one part of draught malt vinegar. Half fill a glass jar or a horizontal wooden barrel depending on the volume of vinegar to be made. The neck of the glass jar or the bung hole of the barrel should be plugged with non-absorbent cotton wool to keep out vinegar flies. If a wooden barrel is used, bore two 2 in. holes in one end just above the level of the vinegar and another two in the end just above the level of the vinegar and another two in the other side but near the edge of the horizontal staves. These holes must also be plugged with non-absorbent cotton wool. The barrel should be fitted with a wooden draw-off tap. A barrel previously used for transporting vinegar is ideal for the purpose.

Leave the jar or barrel in a warm room (90° to 95°F. preferably) for six to eight weeks, or three to six months at lower temperatures, when conversion to vinegar should be complete. This can only be tested in the home by tasting the vinegar, unless one knows a chemistry master or has a son doing chemistry. In such cases the acidity of the vinegar should be over 4 per cent acetic acid. Three-quarters of the vinegar is decanted or run off into clean jars which should be full when corked. Seal the tops of the jars with wax, since if the vinegar comes into contact with air during storage, the bacteria then attack the vinegar itself, turning it into carbon dioxide and water.

Replace the vinegar withdrawn from the jar or cask with an equal volume of cider or diluted wine and repeat the vinegar making. This can be repeated many times providing care is taken in maintaining the necessary warmth.

The storage jar should be kept in a cellar for nine months to clear. If it is then still hazy it should be clarified by adding one tablespoonful of milk to each gallon of vinegar and mixing thoroughly. Allow the precipitate to settle, then carefully syphon off the clear liquid and add two Campden tablets to each gallon of clear vinegar to preserve its clarity.

Home-made Wines, Syrups and Cordials,
The National Federation of Women's Institutes, 1954

Verjuice

Verjuice (literally 'green juice') is the name normally given to the juice distilled from sour crabapples. The word was used in Roman times to describe a kind of grape juice, but from the middle ages onwards it related specifically to crabapples. Up till the time of Shakespeare it was a vital kitchen ingredient, but its use gradually declined; it was superceded by vinegar and also by lemon juice.

Verjuice was a basic component of the highly spiced sauces that were a feature of cookery in the middle ages. With parsley, grapes, egg yolks and garlic it made a sauce for roast goose; for preserving freshwater fish it was combined with saffron and nutmegs, to make a thin yellow broth that was poured over the fish. The sophisticated cooks of the French court had developed these sauces and they gradually became a fundamental part of high English cookery. Verjuice itself resembles dry cider – it is mild and sharp tasting, and its use in sauces with meat and fish may have led to the evolution of dishes more familiar to us, such as herrings baked in cider. By the middle of the sixteenth century verjuice was used as a base for pickles, which indicates that these preserves were very mild compared with those made today from vinegar. Thomas Tusser also noted that verjuice was the best tonic for cattle made feeble by the harsh conditions of winter.

The process of making verjuice is similar to that used for making some types of cider on a small scale. Gather the crabs when they are very ripe and put them in a heap until they 'sweat'. Having removed any rotten fruit, mash the crabs to a pulp in a suitable container. (Traditionally this mashing was done in large troughs using a 'beetle' or large wooden mallet, a tool which is now largely confined to fairground sideshows.) Then strain the juice through a jelly bag. The verjuice should be bottled and stored for about a month before it is ready for use.

Chapter 7

CHUTNEYS, KETCHUPS
AND SAUCES

The word ketchup is derived from the Chinese 'koe-chiap', a pickled
fish sauce that probably originated in China, and was introduced into
south-east Asia and India by travellers and Chinese immigrants.
Chutney too is oriental in origin – the word comes from the Hindustani
'chatni' meaning a strong, sweet relish. Neither of these products
appeared in England until the end of the seventeenth century. But it is
worth mentioning an exceptional recipe from medieval France listed in
The Goodman of Paris, and called 'compost'. It consisted of a mixture of
walnuts, turnips, carrots, choke pears, pumpkins, peaches and the roots

94

of fennel and Hamburgh parsley. To these were added mustard seed, anise, fennel, coriander, caraway seeds, horseradish, cloves, cinnamon, ginger, pepper, grain of Paradise (a spice related to cardamom), nutmeg, saffron, and red cedar. All the ingredients were mixed with honey and raisins, and finally boiled up with quantities of wine. Apart from the list of ingredients, the most interesting aspect of this preserve was the length of time it took to prepare; it was started on St John's Day (24 June) and not completed until after St Andrew's Day (30 November).

It was the increased trade with the Orient carried on by the East India Company from the last years of the seventeenth century that brought ketchups and chutneys to England. Some of the earliest samples to be introduced were soy sauce and 'Piccalilli', an elaborate Indian pickle which was imitated by English cooks as early as 1694 when one book lists a recipe 'To pickle lila, an Indian pickle'. This was a vinegar-based sauce flavoured with garlic, ginger, mustard seed, pepper and turmeric in which were pieces of fruit and vegetables such as cabbage, cauliflower and plums.

About this time, cooks discovered that the liquor left after a jar of pickle had been eaten was useful and worth keeping, and although the oriental 'koe-chiap' – now transformed into catchup – was a fish sauce, these pickle liquors were thought to have similar qualities; they were dark, pungent and spicy. This range of condiments and ketchups became known as 'store sauces', a title used to describe their keeping qualities, and also to distinguish them from sauces made to garnish a particular dish. So the liquor from pickled mushrooms became mushroom ketchup, and other pickles such as walnuts were treated in a similar manner. It wasn't long before anchovies were included in these store sauces to make them more accurate imitations of their oriental counterparts, and special recipes were devised. A good example is Quin's Fish Sauce, which is included in Hannah Glasse's *The Art of Cookery Made Plain and Easy*. The forerunner of this recipe was probably a fish sauce made specifically 'to keep the whole year' listed in her original manuscript of 1747 in the chapter 'For the Captains of Ships'. This contained 24 anchovies, a quart of white wine, a pint of red wine, 10 shallots and a handful of scraped horseradish, as well as lemon and spices. Mrs Glasse described it as a 'pretty sauce' for boiled fowl or veal. It was 'lowered' (diluted) with hot water and thickened with a piece of butter rolled in flour. Quin's Sauce, included in some later editions of the book, was a slightly more tame and economical version of this original fish sauce.

Quin's Fish Sauce

Take quart of walnut pickle put to it six anchovies with mace, cloves and whole pepper, six bay leaves, six shallots, boil them all together till the anchovies are dissolved, when cold put in half a pint of red wine and bottle it up; when you use it give it a shake, two spoonfuls of this to a little rich melted butter makes a good sauce.

The Art of Cookery Made Plain and Easy, / Hannah Glasse, 1796 edition

A glance through any typical nineteenth-century cookery book might suggest that there was an amazing variety of store sauces, but on closer examination it is clear that the only real difference lay in the names and in the proportions of the quite standard ingredients used. These included walnut pickle, shallots, horseradish, anchovies, spices, and sometimes soy sauce and shellfish. They were either named after the establishment where they were supposed to originate, such as Pontac's sauce, or after some individual who imagined that he had created a unique preparation, and thus felt it only right to name the sauce after himself. Harvey's sauce is the most famous of these, and W. C. A. Blew in *The Quorn Hunt and its Masters* gives a revealing account of its true origins. In this case there's more than a hint of sharp practice.

Captain Charles Combers (born 1752), a member of the Quorn Hunt, when on his way to Leicestershire stopped, as was his wont, to dine at The George at Bedford, then kept by a man named Harvey, where he ordered a steak, and when it was served Combers requested Harvey to let his servant bring from his buggy a quart bottle which contained an admirable sauce. Combers poured some of it into his plate and having mixed it with the gravy of the steak he asked Harvey to taste it, and the host pronounced it to be a most excellent relish.

'Well, Mr Harvey,' said Combers, 'I shall leave the bottle with you to use till my return, only be careful to reserve enough for me.'

On the next day Harvey had to provide a wedding dinner, and introduced the sauce which afforded such general satisfaction, that several small parties were made up and the contents of the bottle were soon exhausted. In due course Captain Combers returned, and having been told no more sauce remained, said, 'Never mind, I can make some more from my mother's recipe, and by the by, I'll give you a copy of it.' He did so. Harvey made it in large quantities, sent it to different shops in London; advertised it as Harvey's sauce and by its extensive sale realized a large income – he subsequently sold the recipe for an annuity of £400 or £500 a year.

> Reprinted in *Good Things in England*,
> Florence White, Jonathan Cape, 1932

So Mrs Combers' sauce became Harvey's sauce. The recipe, as made in 1830, included:

12 anchovies; 1 oz. cayenne pepper; 6 spoonfuls soy (sauce); 6 spoonfuls walnut pickle; 3 bulbs garlic; $\frac{1}{4}$ oz. cochineal; 2 shallots; 1 gallon vinegar.

Harvey's sauce was used as an ingredient in even more elaborate sauces such as Christopher North's sauce and Reform sauce, which was devised by the royal chef, Francatelli, who in 1852 became chef at the Reform Club in London; it was a typically excessive mixture of common brown sauce with port, anchovy essence, Harvey's sauce and redcurrant jelly.

By the nineteenth century the fashion-conscious cooks of English families had begun to make 'chatnis' and relishes based on their oriental prototypes. We can get some idea of what these were like from Eliza Acton, who herself obtained information about these foods from 'a highly intelligent medical man who has been for twenty years a resident in the Mauritius'.

The composition of these favourite oriental sauces varies but little except in the ingredient which forms the basis of each. The same piquant or stimulating auxiliaries are intermingled with all of them in greater or less proportion. These are, young onions, chillies, (sometimes green ginger), oil, vinegar, and salt; and occasionally a little garlic or full grown onion, which in England might be superseded by a small portion of minced eschalot. Green peaches, mangoes, and other unripe fruits, crushed to pulp on the stone roller . . .; ripe bananas, tomatoes roasted or raw, and also reduced to a smooth pulp; potatoes cooked and mashed; the fruit of the egg-plant boiled and reduced to a paste; fish, fresh, salted, or smoked, and boiled or grilled, taken in small fragments from the bones and skin, and torn into minute shreds, or pounded, are all in their turn used in their preparation. Mingle with any one of these as much of the green onions and chillies chopped up small, as will give it a strong flavour; add salt if needed and as much olive oil, of pure quality, with a third as much of vinegar, as will bring it to the consistence of a thick sauce. Serve it with currie, cutlets, steaks, pork, cold meat, or a fish, or aught else to which it would be an acceptable accompaniment.

Modern Cookery for Private Families, Eliza Acton, 1845

The impact of the colonial era on cookery was quite considerable and in many cases an interesting two-way traffic developed. A hundred years after Eliza Acton was writing, a recipe for that most English of preparations, Worcester sauce, appears in a book of Mauritian cookery. In fact Worcester sauce was originally developed from a recipe brought to England by an aristocratic gentleman at the beginning of the nineteenth century. As the taste for 'chatnis' developed and the need for fashionable imitations declined, the oil was omitted and sugar was added to make a produce that resembled our present day chutneys. The ingredients altered as well, the most significant change being the widespread use of tomatoes. These were brought back from America by seamen and cultivated around the Mediterranean as early as the sixteenth century. It wasn't until the nineteenth century that they were used extensively in English cooking; since then they have rapidly become one of the most common ingredients of chutneys and ketchups, and today 'tomato sauce' is almost as essential a condiment as salt and pepper on English tables. But the really striking thing about most of today's chutneys and ketchups is their blandness compared with their nineteenth-century predecessors. Commercial chutneys usually have sugar beet as their main ingredient; they are ridiculously over-sweet with a gummy consistency caused by quantities of tragacanth and gum arabic.

CHUTNEYS

Raw materials

Fruit and vegetables: the quality of these is not too important in chutneys, since they are often reduced to a pulp during cooking. As long as they are fresh and sound, the lower grades can be used.

Don't be afraid to try out new combinations of fruit, vegetables and spices. Whilst there are a number of well-tried combinations, there is always the possibility of going beyond recipe and formula, ignoring conventional tastes and creating something new.

Vinegar: malt vinegar is normally used for chutneys. Where a light colour or less intense taste is required, then white vinegar can be substituted. By adding part of the vinegar towards the end of the cooking, the total amount can be reduced.

Spices: these are the most important ingredients. Use them selectively, but be sure to use a sufficient quantity; the blandness of many of today's chutneys is due partly to a lack of enthusiasm for spices. Ground spices are normally used as they are easier to handle, but whole spice gives the chutney a better flavour since it tends to retain its volatile oil during storage. When whole spices are used they should be bruised and tied in a small muslin bag before adding to the chutney mixture, and removed before potting.

Sugar: either white or brown sugar can be used depending on the type of chutney required. Rich, dark chutneys will result from the use of brown sugar, although even a long cooking with white sugar will darken the colour of a chutney. If a light colour is required, the sugar can be added fairly late in the cooking, when the other ingredients have softened. The amount of sugar used can be reduced by adding dried fruit such as raisins, sultanas, dates and crystallized ginger. Honey may also be used; this was a common procedure before sugar was readily available. Nowadays the price of honey has restricted its use, but a few spoonfuls added to some chutneys transforms them.

Points to remember are:

1. All cooking pans should be made of stainless steel or aluminium, and wooden spoons should be used.

2. The eventual quality of a chutney depends to a large extent on cooking and storage. It should be cooked gently for a long time. To ensure proper thickening the cooking should be done without a lid even though this may result in some loss of the volatile oils from the spices. But the crucial stage is storage and maturation. For the best

results the chutney should be kept for months, even years, before it is used.

3. Always bottle the chutney while it is hot. Put into warm, dry clean jars. The jars should be well covered; if not, the chutney will dry out and shrink badly.

The same containers and covers suggested in Pickles (pp. 58-9) can be used for chutneys. The main difference is that waxed paper and plastic covers should be used provided that the chutney can be stored in a completely dry cupboard; the slightest amount of damp will affect the chutney. If you are in any doubt reinforce the cover either with parchment paper, or cloth dipped in melted paraffin wax.

Red Tomato Chutney

It was an unequalled year for tomatoes. There was a glut of them and they were selling for only a few pence a pound, so Rose and I lived off fresh tomato sandwiches and ratatouille – for the first time a dish that we could reasonably afford to make. We also made huge quantities of tomato chutney and passed jars onto our friends.

5 lb. ripe tomatoes; 1 lb. onions; 3 cloves garlic; 2 tsp. salt; 2 tsp. paprika; 1 tsp. cayenne pepper; 2 tsp. crushed mustard seed; 8 oz. sugar; 1 pint white vinegar.

First weigh and peel the tomatoes. If they are ripe they should peel quite easily; if not scald them first. Chop them roughly into pieces and put into a preserving pan with the chopped onions, garlic and a little vinegar. Cook slowly until the tomatoes have turned to pulp and the onions are beginning to feel soft. We like tomato chutney smooth but with pieces of onion that are crisp and succulent, so we cut the onions roughly into fair-sized pieces. At this stage it is sometimes suggested that the mixture should be sieved, but we do not think this necessary. You can smooth out the texture by stirring and pressing with a wooden spoon.

Then add all the other ingredients and continue to cook until the chutney is thick and well-blended. You may need to adjust the quantities of sugar and vinegar if the sweetness and consistency are not absolutely right. This chutney benefits from a long slow cooking, and you should take at least 2 hours over the whole task.

When the chutney is ready it should be bottled and stored for a couple of months before using. It improves with keeping and is extraordinarily versatile; it goes well with meat, fish, cheese (especially in sandwiches of rough home-made bread) and it is useful in meat dishes where tomato purée might otherwise be included.

You can make this chutney even more colourful and interesting by adding some chopped red and green peppers, aubergines and red chillies. It is a dazzling sight as it cooks in the pan, and it has a sublime smell. You will need to adjust the amounts of vinegar and sugar slightly.

Green Tomato Chutney

2 lb. grccn tomatocs; 8 oz. onions; 8 oz. apples; 4 oz sultanas; 1 tsp. salt; $\frac{1}{2}$ tsp. cayenne pepper; $\frac{1}{2}$ tsp. dry mustard; 8 oz. sugar; $\frac{1}{2}$ pint malt vinegar.

Green tomatoes are usually very easy to obtain, and they're much cheaper than ripe red tomatoes. If you grow tomatoes yourself, pick off some of the small green fruit and use them for this chutney. You may also be able to get some from a friend or neighbour, or from roadside stalls during September and October.

It is best to skin the tomatoes before using them. This can be done quite easily by scalding them in boiling water for $\frac{1}{2}$ minute before peeling. (It is not necessary if they are very small.) Chop the tomatoes and put them in a preserving pan with the peeled and chopped apples and onions. Add about half the vinegar and cook gently until the tomatoes and apples are soft, keeping the mixture well stirred. Then add the rest of the vinegar and all the other ingredients and continue to cook steadily until the chutney thickens. This should not take longer than 15 minutes. We have noticed that this chutney has a tendency to dry out, so make sure you don't overcook it; pot while it is still slightly runny and cover.

Orange Chutney

7 large sweet oranges; 1 lemon; 5 large cooking apples; 3 onions; 4 oz.

sultanas; 8 oz. brown sugar; 8 oz. white sugar; 1 tsp. ground black pepper; 2 tsp. ground ginger; 1 tsp. cayenne pepper; 1½ pints malt vinegar.

We discovered this chutney at a party given by a friend. It was very fiery and caused much eye-watering. The whole occasion was quite memorable; after gorging ourselves on crumbly home-made paté, we had cold capon and ham with the chutney. We were saved by a fruit salad made with sliced fresh greengages, and by a supply of wine that never seemed to diminish. We later obtained the recipe, and this is a slightly adapted version of it.

Grate the rinds of the oranges and lemon into a preserving pan, making sure none of the pith is grated as this will make the chutney bitter and unpleasant. Peel the oranges and lemon, cut the flesh into small pieces (removing any pips), and add to the preserving pan. Then peel and chop the apples and onions, add the spices, vinegar and sugar and simmer for about an hour. (Brown sugar gives the chutney a dark colour and smooth, rich taste.) When the chutney has thickened, pot and cover while hot.

Apple Chutney
There are a great number of recipes for apple chutney, some hot and spicy, others like this one, mild, dark and fruity. This was in fact the first chutney Rose ever made. It was several years ago and she was looking after her parents' house while they were away. Rose and a friend had been apple picking, since it was that season and there were orchards near by, and they returned to the house loaded with pounds of windfalls. So they peeled apples and onions, and raided the larder for sugar and vinegar. And they set to work, stirring the ingredients in a huge aluminium preserving pan. When I discovered the chutney nearly two years later, it was in a weird-shaped jar with a makeshift lid. In fact it had kept extraordinarily well, and was one of the most delicious chutneys I had tasted; I used to eat it with every conceivable food.

This is the recipe as Rose remembers it:

3 lb. apples; 3 lb. onions; 1 lb. sultanas; juice and rind of 2 lemons; 1½ lb. demerara sugar; 1 pint malt vinegar.

Peel, core and chop the apples into small pieces, and also peel and chop the onions. Put them in a preserving pan with the sultanas. Then grate the rinds of the lemons, making sure no pith is removed, and squeeze the juice into the pan as well. Add the vinegar and bring to the boil slowly. When the apples have softened add the sugar and continue cooking gently until the chutney thickens. Pot and cover while hot.

Apple and Mint Chutney

2 lb. cooking apples; 1 lb. onions; 8 oz. tomatoes; 4 oz. stoned raisins; 2 tsp. finely chopped mint; 2 tsp. salt; 1 tsp. dry mustard; 1 tsp. cayenne pepper; 8 oz. soft brown sugar; 1 pint malt vinegar.

First prepare all the ingredients: peel and chop the apples, tomatoes and onions, chop the raisins and mint. Put all these into a preserving pan with half the vinegar and cook slowly until soft. Meanwhile mix the mustard and cayenne pepper with a little of the remaining vinegar and add to the pan. When all the ingredients are soft, stir in the sugar, salt and the rest of the vinegar, and boil until the chutney is thick. Allow to cool slightly and then pot and cover.

Like apple chutney, this keeps well and should be stored for at least six months before opening.

Pear Chutney

1½ lb. cored and peeled pears; 8 oz. onions; 8 oz. green tomatoes; 4 oz. stoned raisins; 4 oz. celery; ¼ tsp. cayenne pepper; ¼ tsp. ground ginger; 1 tsp. salt; 12 oz. demerara sugar; 1 pint malt vinegar.

Last summer we had a very good crop of pears, and we decided to make a large quantity of pear chutney using this recipe. At first we were slightly dubious about the use of celery and green tomatoes with pears, but in fact it is an unlikely combination that works surprisingly well.

Peel, core and slice the pears and weigh them; chop the tomatoes, onions and celery. Put all the ingredients except the sugar into a pan and bring to the boil slowly. Simmer until the pears are tender. After the fruit has softened, add the sugar and continue cooking slowly. At

this stage you will need to stir from time to time. When the chutney has thickened, pour into jars and cover.

Mango Chutney

Recipes for mango chutney date back to the nineteenth century, yet the product often did not include mangoes at all; Mrs Beeton used apples as a substitute, and Eliza Acton green gooseberries. Nowadays mangoes are still a relatively expensive fruit in most areas, although they are beginning to appear in some of the better supermarkets, and can often be got quite cheaply in the Indian grocers' shops that are found in some cities. Use unripe fruit for chutney.

8 large mangoes (green); 2 oz. salt; 1 pint malt vinegar; 1 oz. bruised root ginger; 2 sticks cinnamon; 1 oz. mustard seed; 2 tsp. cayenne pepper; 8 oz. sugar.

Peel and slice the mangoes into fairly substantial pieces, put into a bowl and scatter with salt. Leave for 24 hours. When the mangoes have stood for a day, rinse them. Measure out about $\frac{1}{2}$ pint of the vinegar and heat it in a preserving pan with the sugar until a thick syrup is formed, then add the rest of the vinegar and the mangoes. Cook gently for about 10 minutes. Add all the remaining ingredients; put the spices in a muslin bag. The amount of cayenne pepper can be varied according to taste, but this chutney should be syrupy sweet and powerfully hot to have its full effect. Simmer for about $\frac{1}{2}$ hour till syrupy, then pot and cover.

Mango chutney is the Englishman's standard accompaniment to Indian food, and there's really no better use for it.

Lemon Chutney

4 large lemons; 8 oz. onions; 1 oz. salt; 1 pint cider vinegar; 4 oz. sultanas; 1 oz. mustard seed; 1 tsp. ground ginger; 1 tsp. cayenne pepper; 1 lb. sugar.

Wipe the lemons with a damp cloth and chop them up finely, removing the pips. Peel and chop the onions, and put them in a bowl with the lemons. Sprinkle with salt and leave overnight. Next day put the contents of the bowl into a preserving pan (with a very little water if necessary) and simmer until the ingredients are soft. Then add the sugar, spices, sultanas and vinegar; bring to the boil and continue to simmer until a thick consistency is achieved. This usually takes 30–45 minutes. If you do not have a taste for hot, spicy chutneys, the amounts of spice can be reduced, but we feel that products like this need to be sharp and fiery to be truly effective as accompaniments to Indian food.

When the chutney has thickened, it should be spooned into warm jars and covered.

Marrow Chutney

4 lb. peeled marrow pieces; salt; $\frac{1}{2}$ lb. onions; $\frac{1}{2}$ oz. mustard seed; $\frac{1}{2}$ oz. ground ginger; $\frac{1}{2}$ oz. turmeric; $\frac{1}{4}$ oz. cayenne pepper; a few cloves; peppercorns; 3 pints vinegar; 1 lb. sugar.

Choose a good size marrow either from the garden, or from your greengrocer. Peel it and remove the pith. Cut it into pieces and weigh.

Put the marrow in a large dish and strew salt all over it; then leave it overnight.

Next day drain off the liquid and wash the marrow free of excess salt. Put it into a preserving pan with the onions and mustard seed. Mix together the ginger, turmeric and cayenne pepper with a little of the vinegar in a cup, and add to the pan together with the rest of the vinegar. Tie the cloves and peppercorns in a muslin bag and put this in the pan. Bring the whole to a boil slowly, keeping a careful watch on the chutney and stirring occasionally. Then mix in the sugar. Allow the chutney to cook slowly for about an hour.

Don't overcook this chutney otherwise it will dry out after it has been bottled. It should be slightly runny and the pieces of marrow should still be intact. When it is cooked, transfer it hot to jars and cover. (Don't forget to remove the muslin bag before you bottle the chutney.)

This recipe will give you a dark yellow chutney, hot with the pieces of marrow succulent and slightly crisp. It's good with cold meat, and we also use it to accompany curry.

Apricot Chutney

This is a chutney which is equally good made with fresh or dried apricots, but we prefer to use dried apricots for the chutney, and reserve the fresh fruit for eating.

8 oz. dried apricots; 1 lb. apples; 4 oz. sultanas; 2 cloves garlic; juice and rind of 1 lemon; 1 tsp. salt; 3 tsp. pickling spice; 1 pint malt vinegar; 1 lb. dark brown sugar.

Chop the apricots and let them soak overnight in water. Next day, drain them and put in a pan with the chopped apples, sultanas, and all the other ingredients except the sugar and pickling spice. Put the pickling spice in a muslin bag, tie it up and add to the pan. Cook the mixture slowly for about ½ hour, or until the apples are soft, then add the sugar, stir well, and bring the chutney slowly to the boil. Continue boiling until the chutney has thickened; this should take about 15 minutes. When it is cooked, remove the pickling spice, pour it into jars and seal.

This apricot chutney is a rich dark brown colour, very smooth and mild. It doesn't need a long time to mature, in fact it seems to have a better flavour when it is young. It's particularly tasty spread thickly on bread and butter and eaten as a sandwich; in this respect it's more like a jam than a chutney.

Dried Fruit Chutney

8 oz. dried apricots; 8 oz. dried peaches; 4 oz. stoned raisins; 4 oz. dates; 8 oz. onions; 8 oz. cooking apples; 2 cloves garlic; 1 tsp. salt; 1 tsp. ground coriander; $\frac{1}{2}$ tsp. ground cloves; $\frac{1}{2}$ tsp. cayenne pepper; 1 tsp. dry mustard; 1$\frac{1}{2}$ lb. soft brown sugar; 1 pint malt vinegar.

Put the apricots and peaches to soak in a bowl of water for 24 hours. Then drain and chop into small pieces. Peel, core and chop the apples finely as well as the onions, dates, raisins and garlic. Put all these ingredients into a pan with about half of the vinegar, and cook slowly until the fruit begins to feel soft.

Mix the spices and blend with a little of the remaining vinegar until a smooth paste is formed. Then add this with the salt and the rest of the vinegar to the pan. Measure out the sugar and slowly add this, stirring until dissolved. Then bring the mixture to the boil and continue boiling until the chutney is thick and pulpy. It can then be poured hot into jars and covered.

This chutney keeps well and should be stored for several months before using.

Date and Banana Chutney

6 bananas; 8 oz. stoned dates; 8 oz. cooking apples; 1 lb. onions; 2 oz. crystallized ginger; 2 tsp. salt; 1 tsp. ground allspice; 1 tsp. turmeric; 1 tsp. ground ginger; $\frac{1}{2}$ tsp. cayenne pepper; 1 tsp. ground coriander; 8 oz. brown sugar; $\frac{1}{2}$ pint malt vinegar.

Peel and chop the onions and apples and put them into a preserving pan with a little vinegar; cook slowly until soft. Then add the bananas (peeled and chopped), the chopped dates and the crystallized ginger. Blend the spices together and make into a paste with a little vinegar; add to the pan. Continue to cook very slowly until the chutney begins to look thick and pulpy. Then stir in the salt and the sugar, and add the remainder of the vinegar. You may find that you need slightly more than the specified amount of vinegar to prevent the chutney becoming thick and sticky too early. When the chutney is almost ready, bring to the boil for a few minutes, and then pour into jars and cover in the usual way.

Beetroot Relish

1 lb. cooked beetroot; 1 lb. onions; 2 tbs. fresh grated horseradish; 1 tsp. salt; 1 tbs. dry mustard; 1 tsp. white pepper; $\frac{1}{2}$ lb. sugar; 1 pint white vinegar.

Prepare and cook the beetroot in the usual way by boiling in water until they are soft; then peel and chop roughly into small pieces. Put into a preserving pan with the chopped onions and horseradish and half the vinegar; cook until the onions are soft. Mix together the mustard and a little vinegar and add this paste to the pan with the rest of the vinegar, the sugar, salt and pepper. Simmer until the chutney is a good consistency, then bring to the boil for 5 minutes, pour into jars and cover.

This chutney goes well with fish.

Piccalilli

2 lb. mixed vegetables – green tomatoes, onions, cauliflowers, cucumber, marrow, radish pods, nasturtium seeds, etc.; 1 tbs. dry mustard; $\frac{1}{2}$ oz. turmeric; $\frac{1}{2}$ oz. ground ginger; $\frac{1}{2}$ oz. flour; $\frac{1}{2}$ tsp. celery seed; 1 pint white vinegar.

Chop the vegetables into small pieces; very small onions can be left whole; the cauliflower should be divided into small flowerets; the marrow peeled and de-seeded; the radish pods and nasturtium seeds can be left as they are. Sprinkle all these ingredients with salt and let them stand overnight. Dry salt is better than brine since it allows the vegetables to retain their crispness. Next day wash the vegetables free of salt and drain them well. Then mix the mustard, spices and flour together with a little of the vinegar till you have a smooth paste; add the rest of the vinegar and the celery seeds, and boil this mixture in a saucepan for 10–15 minutes, or until the sauce has thickened. Pack the vegetables into jars and pour over the hot mustard sauce so that they are completely covered, and seal.

The quantities and types of vegetables that you include can of course be varied. A sweet version of this relish can be made by adding 2 oz. of brown sugar to every pint of vinegar when making the sauce.

Sweetcorn Relish

The sweetcorn for this relish can be either from fresh or frozen cobs, from packets of frozen corn or from the quite satisfactory tinned variety.

1 lb. sweetcorn (off the cob); 4 oz. chopped white cabbage; 1 green pepper; 1 red pepper; 4 oz. celery thinly sliced; 4 oz. white sugar; 2 tsp. salt; 2 tsp. dry mustard; 1 pint white vinegar.

Prepare the sweetcorn (if fresh or frozen on the cob it will need to be cooked, allowed to cool and the corn stripped off the cob). Chop the cabbage (a fleshy white cabbage is best for this purpose), peppers and celery. Put them in a preserving pan and cook fast for about 5 minutes adding a little water if necessary. Drain off any excess liquid and add the sweet corn. Mix together the sugar, salt and mustard, add a little of the vinegar until a thin paste is formed. Put this and the remainder of the vinegar into the pan with the vegetables, mix well and cook for about 15 minutes after bringing to the boil. Pour hot into jars and seal. This relish may not keep for more than a couple of weeks after it has been opened, so it should be used up quickly.

KETCHUPS AND SAUCES

These comments apply to ketchups and sauces that are made from pulped fruit and vegetables. ('Store sauces' can be treated like pickles as regards preparation and storage.) Much of what we have already said in relation to chutneys also applies to ketchups. The ingredients should be sieved after cooking to give a product with a smooth consistency. Cooking normally takes longer for ketchup so that the fruit tissues are reduced to a pulp and the ketchup will pour satisfactorily. They tend to thicken on cooling.

It is advisable to sterilize ketchups and sauces after bottling since there is always a danger of fermentation, particularly in tomato and mushroom-based sauces. Others which are more acidic are less likely to ferment but it is wise to sterilize all the same.

1. Choose bottles which will withstand the heat needed to sterilize the ketchup. Old sauce bottles with a well-fitting screw cap are ideal. If other bottles are used they can be corked, but the corks must be tied down.

2. Wash the bottles and caps or corks and then boil in water for $\frac{1}{4}$ hour. This is particularly important since corks are likely to go mouldy during storage if not sterilized.

3. Remove the bottles from the water – the long handle of a wooden spoon is a useful tool for this job. Drain out excess water and put onto a wooden surface (not cold marble or tiles).

4. Pour in the hot ketchup using a funnel and fill the bottles to within 1 inch of the top. Lightly seal or cork at once. Then they must be sterilized. The water used in (2) can be used again here. Put the bottles upright into the pan on a false bottom and ensure that the water level comes up to the neck. You can use newspaper padding to keep them upright.

5. Bring the water to the boil and simmer either at 190°F for 20 minutes, or 170°F for 30 minutes. If you do not have a thermometer, let the water bubble vigorously for 15 minutes. You may need to top up with fresh hot water from time to time. The important factor is to maintain the temperature for a sufficient length of time to ensure complete sterilization. Then remove the bottles (remember they will be very hot, so use an oven cloth). Tighten the screw caps or corks securely and leave until cool.

6. To ensure a completely airtight seal, the necks of the bottles, when cold, can be dipped in melted paraffin wax (melted candle wax can be used instead).

7. The ketchup should then be stored in a cool dry place. Once opened a particular bottle will not keep for more than a couple of weeks, so make your ketchup in batches using practical-sized bottles.

Note: the words 'ketchup' and 'sauce' do not have any special significance. Most ketchups consist of pulped fruit and vegetables, and sauces are mixtures of spices and other ingredients infused in vinegar and later strained off, but the terminology is flexible.

Tomato Ketchup

When most people speak of 'ketchup' or 'sauce', this is what they mean. If properly made and used when it suits the meal, it is a marvellous preparation, but too often the ubiquitous bottle is a sure sign of unpalatable food. Sauce bottles line fish and chip shop counters and dominate formica-topped tables in restaurants; and in transport cafes there are plastic globes with spouts blocked by congealed ketchup and grease. Not an atmosphere that suggests good food, yet in some transport cafes you will eat more cheaply and better than in many flamboyant town restaurants and snack bars. One of the great joys of the early morning is to have a pint of tea and a plate of well-fried eggs, bacon and sausages with a good seasoning of tomato ketchup.

The recipe we are including is for a basic ketchup; you can make it more elaborate if you wish, by adding chopped celery, green and red peppers and so on.

6 lb. tomatoes; 1 onion; 3 cloves garlic; 1 tsp. paprika; 1 tsp. cayenne pepper; juice of 1 orange; 1 tsp. salt; 8 oz. white sugar; $\frac{1}{2}$ pint white vinegar.

Peel and chop the tomatoes and put into a preserving pan with the chopped onion and garlic. Cook slowly until the onion is soft and the tomatoes are pulpy. Add all the other ingredients and continue to cook until the mixture has a thick, even consistency. Then either sieve or liquidize until you have a smooth, lump-free ketchup. Remember that it will thicken on cooling. Bottle the ketchup while hot, seal and sterilize. Remove the bottles, tighten the caps and store. If sterilized correctly this ketchup will keep well, but once a bottle is opened it should be stored in the fridge and used up as quickly as possible.

Rhubarb Sauce

3 lb. rhubarb; 8 oz. onions; 2 tsp. salt; $\frac{1}{2}$ tsp. cayenne pepper; 3 tsp. turmeric; 6 cloves; 1 lb. sugar; 1 pint white vinegar.

Choose young ripe rhubarb and cut it into small pieces as for stewing; peel and chop the onions. Put both these ingredients into a preserving pan with a little of the vinegar and cook slowly until they are soft. Then add the cloves (there is no need to put them in a muslin bag as they can be removed when the sauce is sieved), salt, cayenne pepper and turmeric, which should be mixed to a smooth paste with a little vinegar. Continue to cook slowly until all the ingredients are pulpy and then pass the mixture through a sieve. Return the sieved liquid to the pan, add the sugar and the rest of the vinegar and boil for $\frac{1}{2}$ hour or until the sauce is thick but still pours easily.

After bottling, the sauce should be sterilized unless you intend to use it up very quickly.

Walnut Ketchup

This was a popular ketchup when walnuts were more plentiful than nowadays, and most farms had walnut trees growing in orchards and along the edges of fields. There are several ways of making this ketchup, the simplest being to use the vinegar from pickled walnuts which can be transformed with spices and shallots. Then there is Mrs Beeton's ingenious method which used walnut shells as its starting material; these were soaked for 10 days in salt water, then broken up and pressed with a heavy weight to express the juice. The most usual method however makes use of green walnuts which are bruised and the juice mixed with vinegar and spices, and occasionally red wine, anchovies and beer as well. Use young, green walnuts for this recipe.

25 walnuts; 2 onions; 2 cloves garlic; $\frac{1}{2}$ oz. salt; 4 cloves; 2 blades mace; a few black peppercorns; 1 pint malt vinegar; $\frac{1}{4}$ pint red wine (optional).

Bruise and crush the nuts in a bowl and add the chopped onions, garlic, salt and vinegar, making sure the nuts are completely covered. Leave for 10 days, stirring the mixture occasionally.

Then strain off the liquid and boil it with the spices and the red wine for about 15 minutes. Strain once more and pour the hot ketchup into bottles. Cover and store until required.

Mushroom Ketchup

On 25 September 1779, the naturalist and diarist Gilbert White noted in his journal: 'Full moon. No mushrooms have appeared at all this month. I find that the best crop is usually in Aug: & if they are not taken then, the season for catchup is lost. Many other fungi.' The absence of mushrooms at this time was due, according to White, to 'a want of more moisture'. But on 4 October, he was lucky: 'Mushrooms abound. Made catchup.'

When mushroom ketchup was made in the eighteenth century it was usually no more than a concentrated mushroom essence, and salt was used as the preservative. In many of the recipes port wine and brandy were also included; these not only improved the flavour of the ketchup, but helped to preserve it as well. The product made commercially in the nineteenth century was more elaborate, and combined mushrooms with anchovies, shallots, and spices. Judging from the quantities of salt recommended in most of these old recipes, the resulting ketchup must have been almost unpalatable; nowadays vinegar is used as the main preservative.

3 lb. mushrooms; 3 oz. salt; $\frac{1}{2}$ tsp. ground mace; $\frac{1}{2}$ tsp. ground ginger; 1 tsp. ground black pepper; 1 pint malt vinegar; port wine (2 tablespoons or as much as you can spare).

The best mushrooms for making ketchup are large, black and flat. These are ripe and yield a good quantity of highly flavoured juice. If you pick them from the wild, go out on a dry day since mushrooms gathered during or after rain tend to decay quickly and the resulting ketchup does not keep well.

Gather the mushrooms, remove the base of the stalks and wipe the flaps clean. Break them into pieces and sprinkle with the salt, layer by layer in a bowl. Leave overnight. Next day rinse the mushrooms, and mash them up with a wooden spoon. Put them into an earthenware dish with the vinegar and spices; cover and cook in a warm oven for about $\frac{1}{2}$ hour. Then strain the juice through a sieve, add the port wine and pour the hot ketchup into bottles and seal. Put the bottles into a pan of hot water and simmer for $\frac{1}{2}$ hour. This is very important. Like tomato ketchup, the product is likely to ferment if not sterilized after filling the bottles.

Mushroom ketchup is a very useful flavouring for soups, stews and casseroles.

Elderberry Sauce (Pontac's Sauce)

The origins of this sauce go back to the time of the Great Fire of
London. Before the fire there was a hostelry in Lombard Street
called the White Bear where Samuel Pepys first drank Haut Brion. It

was on the site of this tavern that Monsieur Pontac, owner of the château Haut Brion, set up his famous eating house which was renowned for its elderberry sauce. Originally this was a combination of claret and elderberries, but it was later modified by less extravagant cooks who substituted vinegar for the claret. The sauce had a legendary reputation for its shelf-life; it was meant to be stored for seven years before being opened.

1 quart ripe elderberries (off the stalk); ½ pint vinegar; 1 tsp. salt; 4 shallots, minced; 6 cloves; 20 black peppercorns; 2 pieces root ginger.

Collect elderberries when they are fully ripe and hang heavily from the trees. Simply pluck off the bunches as they are, and strip them when you get home. (Don't worry if you have picked more than you need for the sauce; the remainder can always be used up, in some hedgerow jam, for instance.) Put the berries in an earthenware dish with the vinegar, cook slowly at the bottom of a warm oven (250°F) for about ½ hour, then allow them to steep overnight. Next day strain off the juice into a pan, add the minced shallots, salt and spices and boil for about 10 minutes, then strain through a sieve, pour into bottles and seal.

Eliza Acton recommends that this sauce be eaten with fish, and its sharp fruity taste also suits foods like liver very well; try frying a few slices of pig's liver in the sauce with bacon and thyme.

Nun's Sauce

This is an interesting example of a hot, pungent sauce to accompany roast beef. Dark, fiery condiments were characteristic of households in the north of England, and this sauce was made by nuns in a Yorkshire convent more than 100 years ago.

¾ oz. cayenne pepper; 2 tbs. soy sauce; 3 cloves garlic; 1 tbs. anchovies; a few cloves; 3 or 4 shallots; 1 tbs. sugar; 1 qt. vinegar.

Pound all the dry things with the dry sugar, chop and add the onions etc., put into a leadless glazed demijohn with the vinegar and cork lightly. This was then left at the foot of the kitchen stairs for a month, and everyone passing up and down to chapel (twice daily) had to give it a shake. At the end of the month it was strained through muslin into the tall glass bottles in the old fashioned cruet stands.

Food in England, Dorothy Hartley, MacDonald, 1954

Anchovies were originally kept in barrels as a standard kitchen item, and the scrapings from the bottom of these were used for the sauce. Nowadays they are rather costly and come in tins like sardines. We don't buy anchovies especially for these sauces, but use what is left after making a pizza. Keep the sauce in a glass jar while it is steeping and store it in a warm, dry cupboard – remembering, of course, to give it a shake quite regularly.

Worcester Sauce

This is perhaps the most famous of all store sauces. It started life in the nineteenth century as Lord Sandys' sauce, but it was to become widely known as Worcester sauce. The story is that the recipe was given to Mr Lea of Lea and Perrins by Baron Sandys of Worcester, who picked it up when in India. But the recipe went unnoticed for many years and it was not until 1838 that the sauce was manufactured on a very large scale. From then on its reputation soared, and until very recently the manufacturers steadfastly kept the precise ingredients a secret; consequently there have been numerous imitations, and this is one such recipe.

2 oz. shallots; 4 cloves garlic; 2 tsp. fresh grated horseradish; 2 tsp. cayenne pepper; 6 cloves; 4 pieces bruised root ginger; 4 cardamom seeds; 10 black peppercorns; 2 fluid oz. soy sauce; 1 pint malt vinegar; 2 tsp. sugar (optional).

Chop the shallots and garlic roughly and boil them for 15 minutes in the vinegar. Then add all the other ingredients and boil for another ½ hour. Keep the lid on the saucepan during the boiling. Transfer to a wide-mouthed bottle, cover and leave for a month. During this time you should shake the bottle occasionally.

After a month strain the sauce through a fine sieve and re-bottle. It is now ready for use.

There is a great temptation when you have such condiments in the larder to use them indiscriminately, tipping them into every available pot and splashing them onto dishes that have been thoughtfully and accurately constructed. Fortunately Worcester sauce seems to suit a great number of foods, but even so you should use it with restraint.

Nasturtium Sauce

This is essentially a variant of Worcester sauce with nasturtium flowers added.

4 shallots; 3 cloves garlic; 6 cloves; $\frac{1}{2}$ tsp. cayenne pepper; $\frac{1}{2}$ tsp. salt; soy sauce; 1 pint malt vinegar; nasturtium flowers.

Gather as many nasturtium flowers as you can. For 1 pint of vinegar you can use up to $\frac{1}{2}$ pint of flowers. Put these in a large jar after checking for insects. Then chop the shallots and garlic and boil up with the vinegar, salt and spices for 10 minutes. Pour over the flowers while hot. Close the jar and leave for 2 months. Then strain the sauce and add soy sauce to taste. Pour into bottles and cover well.

Chapter 8

JAMS, JELLIES, BUTTERS AND CHEESES

The prototype for many of these preserves was the medieval 'marmelade', made from quinces, honey and spices. This was later made with sugar when this became more common in England, and by the sixteenth century other marmalades were also being prepared from plums, damsons, pears, apples, medlars, strawberries and service berries. The fruit was cooked until soft, and then sieved to a pulp; this was mixed with sugar and boiled until the preserve thickened. All these marmalades were solid and were eaten in lumps as sweetmeats.

Various types of jelly were also quite popular from the sixteenth century onwards. Fruit such as strawberries, raspberries and mulberries were crushed in a mortar with sugar and then boiled up with a mixture of water, rosewater and isinglass. The jelly was then sieved, put into boxes and kept for a year. Like marmalades, these jellies were stiff and solid and bore little resemblance to preserves used nowadays. An alternative method of jelly making used for fruit such as gooseberries and barberries that were rich in pectin, was to boil the fruit, strain it through a linen cloth and then boil it with sugar until it set.

While many of the larger, firm fruit such as plums and apricots continued to be made into marmalades, or preserved whole in syrup, soft fruit were often made into a simple type of preserve by bruising and boiling in sugar syrup without any sieving or straining. This type of preserve came to be known as 'jam'. This first appeared in cookery books around 1718 and both the name and the preserve itself quickly replaced many of the earlier types, although marmalades and whole fruit preserved in syrup were still made in small quantities as special items.

By the nineteenth century large quantities of jam were being made in middle- and upper-class households; a great deal of fruit was grown, or could be bought on markets, and sugar was 'very reasonable in price' by this time. Recipes appeared for a large number of jams made from gooseberries, cherries, damsons, raspberries, strawberries and currants. These were used with puddings, rice, semolina and macaroni; they were eaten with bread, used in tarts and made into fruit sauces to be poured over creamy desserts.

In the last years of the nineteenth century, cheap manufactured jam began to appear in the towns and cities. This was mainly the result of the agricultural depression of the 1870s and 1880s, when farmers were anxious to find new markets for unwanted fruit. These jams were concoctions made from fruit and vegetable pulp with extra colouring and flavouring added. In fact the whole process of jam manufacture was very primitive and potentially dangerous. Charles Booth in his survey of the 1880s, *Life and Labour of the People of London*, gives a frightening description of conditions in the jam factories:

The most wholesale business of all, that of jam-making, is ordinarily the work of men as regards mixing and boiling, and the work of women for filling, covering, and labelling the pots; in some factories women are employed to attend to the boiling, the work being made possible for them by the use of steam. . . . women and girls are often badly burnt, either from the bursting of a jar whilst it is being filled with the boiling liquid, or owing to a slip when conveying heavy loads of scalding jam from the furnace to the cooling-room. This dangerous practice is avoided in the best workshops by the use of a barrel on wheels.

Charles Booth's London, edited by A. Fried and
R. Elman, Hutchinson, 1969

By 1900 the sales of jam were enormous, and it became one of the staple foods of poor families, along with bread, bacon and tea. It is easy to see the attraction of jam: it was, first of all, cheap and offered a sweet, colourful addition to the dreary larder. It was normally eaten on bread, often simply as a substitute for butter, or to make bread and margarine slightly more palatable; like the highly spiced sauces used by medieval cooks to disguise the poor quality of salted meat, jams acted as a distraction, they masked the flavour of the food they covered. The second feature of jam was that it provided an alternative to fresh fruit which poor families could not afford to buy. Jam became a staple food in schools, factories and prisons, in fact in all the institutions where the authorities were unwilling to spend more than a minute sum of money on feeding the poor.

The various types of fruit preserve that have evolved over the years have tended to have fairly specific uses. Jams, for example are now usually spread on bread or toast, or used with desserts and cakes. Jellies are sometimes used in this way, but are more commonly served as accompaniments to meat, poultry and game. There is a strong tradition of serving redcurrant jelly with lamb, rowan jelly with venison and so on. These combinations are based on the old principle of serving an animal with the food on which it lived, or at least with local plants that grew where the animal grazed. Cheeses were developed by the Victorians and are really the descendants of marmalades; they were made from sieved fruit pulp and sugar, boiled together until a thick preserve formed. They were turned out of their jars whole and either sliced and eaten with cold meat, or made into elaborate desserts garnished with nuts, whipped cream and port.

JAMS

1. 'Out, fruit go and gather, but not in the dew.' Thomas Tusser's advice, given in the sixteenth century, still holds good today. The rule

of picking only dry fruit applies to all preserves, but it is particularly important in jams and jellies, where the tendency to decay is greatest.

2. Fruit for jam-making should be as fresh as possible and also just ripe. Over-ripe fruit does not set well because of its low pectin content.

3. The basic principle of jam-making is to have sugar, pectin and acid present in the correct proportions. Pectin occurs in varying amounts in the cell walls of fruit, and when the fruit is boiled it is released into solution. Acid is necessary for the proper extraction of the pectin and for setting. It also improves the colour and flavour of a jam, and helps to prevent sugar crystallizing out after the jam has been made. Sugar is used as the preservative and as a sweetener. It is also necessary for a good set.

Pectin: if all fruits had the same pectin content, jam-making would be a very simple process. But the amount of pectin varies, not only from one fruit to another, but even in each variety, and it depends on the ripeness of the fruit. Fruits rich in pectin which give a good set include apples, gooseberries, blackcurrants, redcurrants, damsons. Fruits giving a medium set include plums, greengages, raspberries, apricots and loganberries. Fruits giving a poor set include strawberries, cherries, blackberries, pears, rhubarb, haws, rowan berries, and vegetables such as marrow and carrots.

Those fruits with a high pectin content make good jam easily. But it is usually necessary to add a little extra acid for those with a medium setting quality. Fruits which are lacking in acid and pectin need an additional source of pectin before they will make a satisfactory jam. The most usual method of doing this is to add fruit that is rich in pectin – thus blackberries and apples are often mixed, and so are strawberries and redcurrants. Either the whole fruit or simply the juice can be used.

Another method of ensuring that a jam sets is to use a commercial pectin extract such as Certo. If this has an advantage over traditional methods it is because the fruit does not need to be boiled to extract the pectin – thus the jam should have a better flavour and there should be more of it for the same amount of fruit. But having made preserves such as strawberry jam by the traditional method and also with Certo, we can find little justification for using pectin extract; it really is not necessary. Remember that the use of Certo requires special recipes, and techniques that are different to those used in traditional jam-making.

Acid: if acid needs to be added, the most convenient source is lemon juice. Other fruit juices such as redcurrant and gooseberry are also useful and occasionally a small quantity of citric acid or tartaric acid is added.

Sugar: this is important as it is the preservative in jams. It also affects the setting quality of the preserve – too much or too little sugar will give a poor set. A jam with too little sugar does not keep well, but one with too much is likely to be over-sweet for most people's taste.

4. Jam pans should be made of aluminium or stainless steel, and it is a mistake to try and make too much jam at one session. Aim to have the pan half full after the sugar has been added.

5. The first stage in jam making is to cook the fruit. It should be simmered gently for some time to soften it and to break down the cell walls. It may be necessary to add a little water to prevent burning if the fruit is hard and needs a good deal of cooking. Soft fruit such as raspberries and strawberries do not require any water. It is important to extract as much pectin as possible without overcooking the fruit.

6. When the fruit has cooked sufficiently, the sugar is added. It may be an advantage to warm it before adding it to the pan as it dissolves more quickly when hot. The jam should be well stirred until the sugar is completely dissolved; then the heat can be increased and the jam brought to the boil quickly and allowed to remain boiling. Do not add the sugar too soon or the jam will take too long to reach setting point and will deteriorate in quality.

7. There are several ways of telling when the setting point has been reached, but first you must watch the jam for what is called a 'rolling boil', that is a bubbling activity in the jam that cannot be stirred out. It is something that you can only recognize by experience, but it is a useful indicator that the jam is near to setting. You should then do a simple test. Remove a very small quantity of the jam with a wooden spoon and put a drop onto a cold plate. As it cools the jam should begin to solidify and the surface should crinkle when pushed with a finger. If this occurs the jam is ready. While you are doing the test do not

continue to boil rapidly otherwise you may pass the setting point. If the test is negative continue to boil and test. Another reliable method is to use a jam thermometer. This should be put into hot water before immersing in the jam and the jam should be well stirred before the temperature is read. Make sure the bulb does not touch the bottom of the pan or you will get a false reading. If the jam is boiled to 220°F it will set; occasionally 221°F or even 222°F may give a better result.

There are other tests which rely on determining the sugar concentration in the jam by its weight or volume, but these are laborious and messy compared with the simplicity of the cold plate test.

8. After the jam has reached setting point it should be taken off the heat and any scum removed with a perforated spoon. The jam should then be poured hot into jars which are clean, dry and warm.

If the jam contains a considerable amount of solid fruit, it should be allowed to cool a little and then stirred to disperse the fruit before pouring into the jars; this prevents the fruit from rising to the top of the jam.

9. After the jars have been filled they must be covered. The simplest and most effective way is to use standard jam pot covers. Lay the waxed circle carefully on to the surface of the jam, making sure it is completely covered. Then put on the transparent cover and secure with a rubber band.

Store the jam in a cool, dry, dark cupboard, where it should keep satisfactorily. If you notice mould on the jam for any reason, don't throw the whole jar away; the great majority of moulds are harmless, however unpleasant they may look. Simply spoon off the top layer of jam carefully, and use up the rest of the jar quite quickly.

Quince Jam

'Marmelade of quinces' was the choice preserve of the middle ages. The product was thick and very sweet and was often cut into pieces like a cheese. In fact it was very similar to the Spanish quince paste 'membrilo' and French 'cotignac' which also includes oranges. The recipe given in *The Goodman of Paris* is a splendid example of the medieval 'marmelade':

. . . take quinces and peel them, then cut them into quarters and take out the eye at the end and the pips, then boil them in good red wine and then let them be run through a strainer; then take honey and boil it for a long time and skim it and afterwards set your quinces therein and stir them well up and boil until the honey is reduced to half the amount; then cast therein powdered hippocras, and stir it until it is quite cold, then cut it into pieces and keep it.

The Goodman of Paris, edited and translated by
E. Power, Routledge, 1928

Later, in the eighteenth century, there were two distinct preserves made from quinces – a 'red marmelade' and a 'white marmelade' – which were prepared by elaborate but quite different processes. Compared to these preserves, today's quince jam seems quite simple.

2 lb. quinces (after preparation); 3 lb. sugar; juice of 1 lemon; water.

First prepare the quinces by peeling, coring and chopping into small pieces. Then put them in a saucepan with enough water to cover them; cook slowly until the fruit is soft – this takes 20–30 minutes. Then add the sugar and lemon juice, bring to the boil and continue to cook until setting point is reached. Pot and cover.

Strawberry Jam
It is only worth making strawberry jam if you can get a good supply of fresh fruit from your own garden or direct from the strawberry fields themselves. Even though we have a good patch that would easily provide us with sufficient fruit for jam and for eating, we use all our home crop fresh, and go out strawberry picking for the jam fruit. This is partly a sentimental approach to our own produce. We believe that these strawberries should be enjoyed fresh picked from the plants, as we lie out on the lawn in the hot afternoons of June and July. With the prospect of occasions like this, it's hard to save the fruit for the preserving pan.

The strawberry has been very resilient to change. Although the plant breeders have made it bigger, redder and generally more tempting, without actually improving its flavour, they haven't yet found a way of eliminating the strawberry picker. The plants still grow on the ground, and the fruit, which ripens at different times, still has to be harvested by hand. (The awkward, inaccessible apple tree is already doomed to be replaced by something like a glorified tomato plant, so it is possible that the end of strawberry picking may not be far off.) Of course, it's difficult to convince the economists and plant biologists that there's more to the fruit than simply its profit potential. Although the fruit they produce *looks* tempting, don't be fooled; for all their pretensions they have less flavour than those tiny wild strawberries which cling to the roadside banks. So if you have a choice, go for the smaller, less perfectly formed fruit.

Strawberry picking is uncomfortable; it's hot sweaty work, and until you have experience you won't earn much money. Traditionally picking was done mainly by local women, often farmer's wives, with organized itinerant workers at some of the bigger farms. Nowadays it's becoming more of a family occasion, especially at weekends. The style of picking varies depending on the destination of the crop. If the fruit is to be sold in bulk for processing then picking is simple and quick; the strawberries are 'plugged', that is picked leaving the central pithy core. For sale fresh the process is more tricky, the strawberries must be handled as little as possible and packed carefully in punnets. In this case the fruit is nipped at the stalk about half an inch from the fruit.

Strawberries are rather lacking in acid and pectin, so this has to be added when making jam. It is important to cook the fruit for no longer than is necessary to release its pectin, otherwise the strawberries lose their shape, and the jam is little more than a flavoured pulp. Small, firm fruit are thus an advantage when making strawberry jam.

(1) 7 lb. hulled strawberries; 6 lb. sugar; juice of 2 lemons.

Quickly wash and clean the strawberries. Put the fruit in the preserving pan with the lemon juice, and heat gently with careful stirring. (The lemon juice provides pectin and acid, but may not be necessary with the more acid varieties of strawberry.) Add the sugar and boil until setting point is reached. Then remove the scum and allow the jam to cool a little before pouring into jars. Give it a good stir so that the fruit is well dispersed; it will then remain suspended rather than rising to the surface of the jam. Pot and cover while still warm and store in a dry place.

(2) 6 lb. strawberries; 6 lb. sugar; $\frac{3}{4}$ pint of redcurrant or gooseberry juice.

In this recipe the fruit juice is used as an extra source of pectin and acid. Gooseberry juice is probably the more practical since gooseberries and strawberries are ripe at about the same time, before redcurrants. You can use some of the juice from the preparation of gooseberry jelly for this purpose. First heat the strawberries and sugar in a preserving pan until the sugar is dissolved and the strawberries are soft but not mushy; in this jam they should remain almost intact. Add the gooseberry or redcurrant juice and boil until the setting point is reached. Don't add the juice earlier than this or it will cook too long and lose its effectiveness. Then partly cool, as in recipe (1) and pour the jam into jars.

Rhubarb and Ginger Jam
2 lb. prepared rhubarb; 2 lb. sugar; juice of 2 lemons; $\frac{1}{2}$ oz. bruised root ginger.

Clean and trim the rhubarb and cut it into pieces. Put it into a bowl with the sugar, layer by layer, add the lemon juice and allow to stand overnight. Next day put the rhubarb and the syrup that has formed into a preserving pan and add the ginger tied in a muslin bag. Bring to the boil and continue to cook until the jam has a good consistency and reaches setting point. Remove the muslin bag, then pot and cover while hot.

Rhubarb and Mixed Peel Jam
2 lb. rhubarb; 2 lb. sugar; 4 oz. mixed peel.

Use ripe pink rhubarb for this jam. Clean it and chop into small pieces and put it into a dish with the sugar and mixed peel, layer by layer. Leave overnight. Next day strain off the syrup and boil it up for about 10 minutes. Pour over the fruit and leave for another 24 hours.

After this time both the rhubarb and the peel should have softened, and the syrup should be thick. Transfer both fruit and syrup to a preserving pan and simmer for about $\frac{1}{2}$ hour or until the jam is thick and pulpy. You will need to keep a close watch on the mixture. When it is ready pot and cover in the usual way.

This is a most unusual jam with a sweet scent and a distinctive orange flavour.

Hedgerow Jam

This is a jam that blends the flavours of the autumn hedgerows – blackberries, elderberries, sloes, crabapples, and if you are lucky, hazelnuts. Gathering the fruit is a lengthy process but on a bright September morning a slow excursion down lanes and across heaths is a pleasing way to pass the time. As we had a friend staying with us during last year's jam season, we enlisted his help for a collecting session, a four-mile round trip on foot, and we set out after breakfast with an assortment of bags and baskets.

There weren't any problems in finding quantities of fruit, and by the time we reached the next village it was midday, so we stopped for a while in the pub. After three pints and two pickled eggs, we decided that we had better move on and finish our task, as the sky indicated rain. Typically the clouds passed over, the weather cleared and we arrived home sweating from the heat of the sun.

It had been a very successful and enjoyable expedition, but we still needed elderberries and blackberries. So first we had to make a short journey to pick some elderberries, and then up to the heath behind our house where the best blackberries grow.

Now for the jam:

1 lb. elderberries; 1 lb. blackberries; 1 lb. crabapples; 8 oz. sloes; 4 oz. hazelnuts (optional); 3½ lb. sugar; 3 pints water.

Wash the fruit; remove the stalks from the sloes and prick them with a needle; peel, core and chop the crabapples. Then put all the prepared fruit (blackberries, elderberries, sloes and crabapples) in a pan with the water. If you have managed to collect some hazelnuts, these should be shelled and put in the pan with the fruit. Simmer till soft, add the sugar and continue to stir until it is dissolved. Boil rapidly to set.

The sloes are essential to the overall taste of the jam, but their stones have to be extracted when it is cooking, and this is very tricky. Even with the keenest eyesight you will be lucky to remove all of them, so you must remember to look out for the odd sloe stone when you first bring the jam out. Sieving is a possibility, but it so alters the special texture of the jam with its chunks of crabapple and whole elderberries which burst when the jam is spread on buttered bread, that we don't recommend it.

If you don't have all the ingredients for this jam, you can make a simpler version using only blackberries and elderberries.

Damson and Apple Jam

2 lb. damsons; ½ pint water; 1 lb. peeled and cored cooking apples; 2½ lb. sugar.

Wash the damsons and remove any stalks. Then split the skins lengthways with a knife, put the fruit into a preserving pan with the water and simmer until soft. As this happens you will be able to remove the stones with a wooden spoon. By starting the process in a preserving pan, which has a large surface area, this operation is made much simpler. When you have removed as many stones as possible, add the chopped apple and simmer until this is soft, but not completely mushy; it is best to have some pieces of apple intact in the jam. Then stir in the sugar and boil rapidly until setting point is reached. Pot and cover in the usual way.

Raspberry Jam

Raspberries nowadays are an expensive and treasured fruit; consequently raspberry jam is hardly worth making unless you are lucky enough to obtain a plentiful supply. If you have some perfect, fresh-picked raspberries then the best method is to make this uncooked jam.

(1)   2 lb. raspberries; 2 lb. sugar.

Put the sugar into a fireproof dish and warm gently in the oven. The dish should be placed on the bottom shelf with the oven at about 200°F. Check the sugar frequently; it should be taken out of the oven when it is warm. Add the raspberries to the sugar, mash them well and stir until the sugar has dissolved and blended with the fruit. Pot and cover in the usual way. This jam should be used within a month.

Alternatively the jam can be made in the more usual manner. Eliza Acton recommends that the fruit be combined with currant juice.

(2)   4 lb. raspberries; $1\frac{1}{2}$ lb. currant juice; 3 lb. sugar.

This recipe can be used for either red or white raspberries, with currant juice 'of the same colour'. The raspberries and currant juice should be boiled together until the fruit is soft and mushy. The pan is then removed from the heat, the sugar is added and stirred until it is dissolved. Return to the heat and boil for about 10 minutes stirring well. Pot and cover.

Loganberry Jam

The loganberry originated in America. It appeared in 1881 in the garden of Judge J. H. Logan at Santa Cruz, California, and was thought to be a natural cross between the American dewberry and a variety of red raspberry. It has been grown in this country since about 1900, but it is not found in the wild. However, where the fruit is grown commercially, mainly in southern and eastern England, Worcestershire and Herefordshire, you can usually go and pick some of the crop for your own use quite cheaply. The fruit is ripe during July and August; for jam choose berries that are still bright red – almost ripe – rather than those that are fully ripe and dark purple.

2 lb. loganberries; 2 lb. sugar.

This is a very simple jam to make; there are few problems. Pick the loganberries on a dry day, throw out any bits of leaf or stalk, wash and weigh the fruit. Put into a preserving pan and cook very slowly until the berries are tender. Add the sugar and stir till dissolved. Then boil fast until setting point is reached. Pot and cover in the usual way.

Interesting variations on this recipe can be obtained if you add other fruit, such as cherries, raspberries or redcurrants (useful if you do not have a great quantity of loganberries). The recipe is the same in all cases – use equal quantities of fruit and sugar.

Gooseberry Jam
The first gooseberries of the year are a welcome sight. Our garden with its fruit bushes and trees seems to develop so slowly, and we wait patiently for the whiskered, green berries which are a sure sign that summer has arrived. For jam-making use gooseberries that are green, firm and slightly under-ripe.

(1) 4½ lb. green gooseberries; 6 lb. sugar; 1½ pints water; 12 heads of elderflowers.

Top and tail the fruit – this is most easily done with scissors rather than a knife. Wash them and put into a saucepan with the water. Bring to the boil and allow them to simmer until the fruit is soft, but not over-cooked. Add the sugar, stirring until dissolved, then boil the jam. At this stage add the elderflowers. There are various methods of doing this, perhaps the most attractive being simply to draw the elderflower heads in turn through the cooking jam, holding them by the stalk. This gives the jam a subtle impression of elder – more scent than flavour. Alternatively the flower heads can be put into a muslin bag and this added to the jam. It's worth testing the flavour as cooking progresses, until a satisfactory blend of flavours is achieved. Boil the jam until a rolling boil is obtained and continue cooking to set, skimming the jam before pouring it into jars.

You can also make gooseberry and orange jam in a similar way. Simply add the juice of 2 oranges to every 3 lb. of gooseberries at the same time as you put in the sugar. This combination is delicious – the sharp flavour of the oranges perfectly offsets the mildness of the gooseberries; this gives the jam a surprising tang.

(2)   This is an old Scottish recipe called Cut Gooseberry Preserve. Choose unripe gooseberries neither too hard nor too soft, top and tail them and cut them in half straight across. Then scoop out the seeds using the wrong end of a teaspoon. This is a fairly tedious task, and is best done by a whole family or a group of friends; it then ceases to be a chore. When the gooseberries are prepared, put them into a saucepan and cover with water. Cook gently for about 30 minutes, and then strain through a sieve or muslin bag. Weigh the gooseberries and for each pound add 1 lb. of sugar, and cook for a further hour or so until the preserve is a good colour and has reached its setting point; then pot and cover in the usual way.

The eventual colour of both these jams depends not only on the variety and maturity of the fruit, but also on the cooking time; the longer the fruit is boiled the redder the jam will be.

Chestnut Preserve

Chestnuts, the fruit of the sweet chestnut (*Castanea sativa*), are autumn's harvest and a feast at Christmas. Go out on a bright Sunday afternoon in late October or November, and if you are lucky the trees will have thrown their green-cased nuts onto the ground. Versatility is one of the virtues of the chestnut. Eaten raw it sustains you while you are gathering; what you bring home can be roasted, turned into marrons glacés, puréed or made into a preserve.

2 lb. chestnuts; 1½ lb. sugar; ½ pint water; 2 tsp. vanilla essence.

Boil the chestnuts in a little water until they are tender – it is a good idea to slit the skins with a knife first. Then peel them and either press through a sieve or roughly grind them in a liquidizer. Depending on your taste you can have a smooth or a rough-textured preserve; we think a rough texture suits the chestnut best. Dissolve the sugar in the water, add the vanilla essence and boil until a thick syrup is formed; put in the chestnuts and continue cooking until the preserve reaches a firm consistency. Pot and cover in the usual way. It is important to store this preserve in a completely dry place as it does not keep for a very long time. So make it just before Christmas and use, not as a sweet preserve spread on bread, but as an accompaniment to cold turkey on Boxing Day evening.

Dried Fig and Rhubarb Jam
1 lb. dried figs; 8 oz. rhubarb; juice of 1 lemon; 8 oz. sugar.

Use thin pink sticks of rhubarb. Chop them into small pieces and put into a bowl with the chopped figs and the lemon juice. Cover with the sugar and leave overnight. Next day put all the ingredients into a pan and bring to the boil slowly. Continue to simmer until the jam is thick and has an even pulpy consistency. Then pot and cover in the usual way.

Cherry and Walnut Jam
This is best made with black cherries, and is more in the nature of a conserve as the fruit is kept intact and extra ingredients are added.

2 lb. black cherries; 1½ lb. sugar; juice of 1 lemon; 4 oz. raisins; 2 oz. chopped walnuts.

Split the cherries and remove the stones, which you should put into a muslin bag. Then put the cherries and the raisins into a preserving pan with a very small amount of water and the bag of stones. Simmer gently until the fruit is soft. Then remove the muslin, add the lemon juice and the sugar; when this has dissolved boil until setting point is reached. At this stage stir in the chopped walnuts, allow the jam to cool a little, then pot and cover.

Marrow Jam

The problem with marrow jam is the condition of the marrow itself. While the best flavour comes from a large, late vegetable, the quality tends to be rather inferior – the flesh is tough and stringy and does not soften easily. Most methods simply involve steeping the cut marrow pieces in sugar before boiling, but we find that this makes for a disappointing jam. As an alternative try the following recipe:

3 lb. prepared marrow; 3 lb. sugar; juice of 3 lemons; 1 oz. bruised root ginger.

First peel the marrow, remove the pith and cut into cubes. Then place the pieces in a steamer and steam until just tender. After cooking put the marrow into a bowl with the lemon juice and the sugar. Leave overnight. Next day transfer to a preserving pan, add the ginger tied in a muslin bag and cook gently until the marrow is soft and transparent, and the syrup thick. Then remove the muslin bag, pot and cover.

Marrow and Pineapple Jam

2 lb. prepared marrow; 1½ lb. sugar; 1 small tin of pineapple.

You must use a young marrow for this recipe. First peel it and remove the pith and seeds, then cut it into small cubes, put it into a bowl and strew with sugar. Leave overnight. Next day transfer the marrow and syrup, a pale golden colour, to a preserving pan. Strain the juice from the tin of pineapple, as this is not required, cut the pieces up if they are too large and add them. Then bring to the boil, slowly stirring, and watching the jam closely. It is easy to overcook this jam so be careful – the presence of the pineapple means that it may easily become hard and sticky. The jam should be cooked until the pineapple is soft and the jam sets when tested. Allow the jam to cool a little, give it a stir to disperse the fruit, then pot and cover.

This jam is particularly useful as a filling for tarts and pastries.

Carrot Jam

carrots; sugar; lemon juice and rind; blanched almonds; brandy.

Peel and chop the carrots into smallish pieces and cook in a little water until tender. Drain off the water and liquidize; measure the volume of pulp and for each pint use the following:

1 lb. sugar; juice and rind of 1 lemon; ½ oz. finely chopped almonds; 1 tbs. brandy.

Put the pulp into a preserving pan with the sugar and lemon juice and boil until the jam is thick. Then add the almonds and brandy, stirring well. Allow the jam to cool a little, give it a good stir to disperse the almonds, then pot and cover. This jam does not keep well without the addition of brandy.

JELLIES

A good jelly is formed when pectin, acid and sugar are present in the correct proportions. Fruits that are high in acid and pectin will make a well-set jelly; others can be transformed by the addition of another pectin source such as apples or redcurrants.

1. The fruit should be fresh, sound and ripe. When making a jelly it is not necessary to remove the stalks from currants or to peel and core apples so long as the larger pieces of stem and any leaves are removed. Wash the fruit before cooking.

The first stage in jelly-making is to cook the fruit until it is tender. This is done by simmering it in a large saucepan or preserving pan for between ½ hour and 1 hour; soft juicy fruit such as blackberries do not take long to cook and only a little water needs to be added, mainly to prevent the fruit from burning in the pan. Other harder fruit should normally be covered with water, and take longer to soften. You can help this process along by stirring and pressing with a wooden spoon. Don't be tempted to rush this stage as it is vital to the formation of a good jelly. The fruit must be broken down sufficiently to release acid and pectin which dissolves in the water. If the fruit is not cooked long enough, the level of pectin and acid will be low and it will be difficult to obtain a good set.

2. When the fruit is well cooked, the juice should be strained off. By far the easiest way of doing this is with a jelly bag. It is possible to

improvise an arrangement using old stockings or muslin, but the jelly
bag is undoubtedly the simplest and least frustrating method of
straining. It can be hooked across the legs of an upturned chair, which
is rested on a second chair, but we find that the edge of the table is the
best place as it is a perfect height for working.

Before using the jelly bag scald it in boiling water. Then put in the pulp and allow it to drip into a bowl.

If the fruit is very rich in pectin, such as blackcurrants, redcurrants or gooseberries, two extractions can be made. The pulp is returned to the pan after straining, mixed with about half the original quantity of water used and re-boiled. It can then be strained a second time.

3. Measure the volume of juice and put it into a preserving pan. Whilst it is generally true that 1 pint of juice and 1 lb. of sugar will make a satisfactory jelly, there are exceptions when less sugar is needed. This depends on the pectin content in the fruit.

First bring the juice to the boil and then add the sugar, stirring until it is dissolved; continue boiling until setting point is reached, stirring occasionally. You can test for a set in the same way as for jam, either by using a thermometer or by dropping a sample of the hot jelly onto a plate: if a skin forms and the spot of jelly becomes tacky, then setting point has been reached and you can go on to pot the jelly. It might be advisable to combine the thermometer reading with the spot test at first, although the difficulties of gauging a setting point are too often over-emphasized.

4. When you have a good set, the pan should be immediately removed from the heat, and the scum taken off with a wooden spoon. The jelly should be poured into jars which have been thoroughly washed, cleaned and warmed, either under a low grill or in the oven. Pour the jelly into the jars carefully to avoid air bubbles.

5. Cover the pots while the jelly is still hot. Ordinary plastic jam pot covers with a piece of waxed paper covering the jelly itself are in most cases perfectly satisfactory, so long as the jelly can be stored in a completely dry place. Once covered the jar should not be moved until it is cold.

6. Ideally the jelly should be kept in a cupboard that is cool and completely dry. If you are in doubt, then the cover should be reinforced using paraffin wax and parchment paper.

Rowan Berry Jelly

Any product with a name like 'rowan berry jelly' is bound to invite jokes; Rose's invention, and the title we now use, was Round Belly Jerry. It is as sumptuous as it sounds.

The bright orange berries of the rowan or mountain ash (*Sorbus aucuparia*), are unmistakable on the trees neatly planted by town councils and on those that grow on heathland. You will need to be quick if you pick from the wild trees, for as soon as the berries have turned orange they are stripped by birds. Town trees seem less susceptible – perhaps even birds respect the by-laws! There are still berries on these in November or December, long after the heathland trees have surrendered their fruit.

The berries are rather dry and lacking in pectin, so it is best to add a few crabapples to compensate. Pick the rowans in clusters, like elderberries, and also collect some crabapples. The more crabapples you add the stiffer your jelly will be. A useful blend is:

1 lb. rowan berries; $\frac{1}{2}$ lb. crabapples; sugar; water.

Put the berries and the chopped crabapples in a pan with enough water to cover them. This prevents burning. Cook till the fruit is soft and strain. Add 1 lb. of sugar to every pint of juice and boil till set. You may find that it takes a long time to reach setting point.

Rowan jelly is bright red with a smoky aroma and a slightly bitter taste. Traditionally it is served with mountain meat such as grouse, venison and mutton, in the same way that redcurrant jelly is paired with the valley meat like lamb. We understood the combination well when we saw deer in the Scottish highlands, stalking nervously among trees and bracken, and rubbing their bodies against the slender trunks of the rowans.

Blackcurrant Jelly

She made a share-cropping deal with Mrs. Curtis, to harvest her currants. She and Peter were going to pick the currants, make jelly out of them, and give Mrs. Curtis half. Four years ago, his mother had bought jelly glasses in the grocery store. Now, the storekeeper shook his head emphatically. 'Don't get any call for them.' It was the bean pot motif, developed. With jelly glasses, naturally, paraffin had gone. And Mason jars with rubbers. 'Haven't had a call for them in years, ma'am. Don't know as they make 'em any more. Guess you notice changes.' 'Yes, I do,' said Peter's mother coldly. 'It's not his fault,' Peter whispered, excruciated.

She was going to make jelly, she said, gritting her teeth, if she had to buy store jelly and dump it down the sink, to use the jars. The thought of this waste sickened Peter; he would rather have gone scavenging in the town dump for old mayonnaise containers. Fortunately, jelly glasses and paraffin were found at the county seat – the glasses covered with dust and cobwebs like some vintage wine.

Birds of America, Mary McCarthy, Weidenfeld & Nicolson, 1966

Blackcurrants are so rich in pectin and acid that they invariably make a very good jelly. If you pick the currants yourself there's no need to strip them from their stalks, but simply use the 'strings' as they are, remembering to give them a wash before starting to make the jelly.

2 lb. blackcurrants; 1 pint water; sugar.

Simmer the fruit in a preserving pan with the water until it is soft; mash well with a wooden spoon during the cooking. Then strain through a jelly bag. Allow the juice to drain for about $\frac{1}{2}$ hour, and then put the pulp from the jelly bag into the preserving pan once more with 1 pint of water and simmer again. Strain and add this juice to the first extract. (This method of making two extracts is a useful way of increasing the yield and so making the jelly more economical. It can only be applied to fruits like blackcurrants which are very rich in pectin and acid.) When the two extracts are mixed together, measure the total volume, and put into the preserving pan with 1 lb. of sugar for each pint of juice. Stir in the sugar when the blackcurrant juice has come to the boil and then continue boiling until setting point is reached.

Blackcurrant jelly has many uses, some familiar, some unjustly neglected. The basting of roast meat seems to have gone out of fashion since the days of the turning spit, but a mixture of blackcurrant jelly, melted and mixed with orange juice and a little mustard, can be cautiously basted over lamb or mutton. There is also an odd American sauce for ham made from the jelly and mustard mixed together.

Red and White Currant Jelly

There are red and white currant bushes in our garden. As the crop ripened last summer we watched and waited impatiently. No doubt the birds watched too, for in July they came, attracted by the shiny red berries and stripped the stalks. There weren't enough redcurrants left to make jelly, so we salvaged what we could and mixed them with some of the whitecurrants that hadn't been touched. Part of the craft of preserving lies in the ability to adapt recipes and products when circumstances require it; new ideas develop out of necessity.

Gather the red and white currants when they are ripe; the proportion of each is not important. Put them in a saucepan to boil with 1 pint of water per pound of fruit. When the fruit has softened strain it through a jelly bag. Measure the volume of juice and transfer it to a preserving pan. Add 1 lb. sugar per pint of juice, stir until it is dissolved, then boil until a good set is obtained. Pot and cover in the usual way.

This mixed jelly has a milder, less sharp taste than the red currant alone. It is very good with roast meat such as leg or shoulder of lamb, and is suitable as an ingredient of Cumberland sauce and other similar sauces.

Sloe and Apple Jelly

Sloes, the fruit of the blackthorn (*Prunus spinosa*), aren't easily picked; the thorns rip your clothes and scratch unprotected arms, and sloe thickets which are common along hedgerows and in woods conceal their fruit. The round, dark blue berries nestle underneath the leaves, and you need a hawk's eye to spot them. The easiest way is to look up into the bush from below.

While the best sloes are those that are picked after the first autumn frosts, their comparative scarcity, and their attractiveness to birds, means that you will have to pick them as soon as you notice the berries. Tasted raw they are too sour to be edible, but the bitter flavour makes for a tangy jelly, clear and dark wine-red coloured. You will need to add apples to the sloes as they are low in pectin, and do not produce a good set on their own.

1 lb. sloes; 1 lb. apples; water; sugar.

When you have gathered your sloes wash them, and if picked before the frost, prick them with a needle. Chop up the apples – there's no need to peel or core them as the juice will be strained off later. Put the sloes and apples in a pan with sufficient water just to cover them, and simmer until they are quite soft. You may need to encourage this by stirring and bruising the sloes with a wooden spoon as they are very hard and troublesome to cook. Strain the juice through a jelly bag. Don't be tempted to hurry the process along by squeezing the bag as this will produce a cloudy jelly. Measure the volume of juice extracted and for each pint add 1 pound of sugar, and heat both in a preserving pan until the sugar has dissolved. Boil fast to set, pot and cover.

Sloe and apple jelly can be eaten with many types of meat and is especially good with mutton, rabbit and jugged hare.

Bramble Jelly

Almost everybody enjoys picking blackberries. They're easy to find, and quite unmistakable, so there are no fears of eating something deadly, and they can be turned into a marvellous jelly. But here people's tastes vary; some like a well-set jelly, but we enjoy it when it is hardly set at all, and can be poured out of the jar – a dripping substance to be spread on thickly buttered bread. But it is no accident that the jelly can seem to be half-set; blackberries are lacking in pectin and acid, both essential to the process of setting, so lemon juice must be added to compensate. By ignoring the lemon juice, the jelly can be made in this strange form.

4 lb. blackberries; juice of 2 lemons (optional); ½ pint water; sugar.

When you have gathered enough blackberries, take them home and wash them well. Then put them in a preserving pan with the water and cook slowly until they are really soft. They should be stirred and pulped with a wooden spoon during cooking. When they are ready, strain through a jelly bag, and for each pint of juice add 1 lb. of sugar, and stir in the preserving pan (with the lemon juice if required), until the sugar is dissolved. Then boil to set, pot and cover.

An alternative method is to add apples to the blackberries. This will guarantee a well-set jelly, as apples are a good source of pectin. Use 2 lb. of chopped apples for every 4 lb. of blackberries, cook the two together until soft, and proceed in the normal way.

Haw Jelly

This is probably the most difficult jelly of all to make satisfactorily. The problem is that haws are so lacking in acid and pectin that even with the addition of lemon juice the jelly simply does not set, but produces a sticky unmanageable gum. If the jelly does set, then by the time it is cold the sugar has crystallized out and you are left with something like a block of sugar candy. The one way to make the jelly successfully is to provide a good source of pectin, such as crabapples, and allow the haws to give their own flavour to this.

2 lb. haws; 2 lb. crabapples; juice of 1 lemon; water; sugar.

Gather haws and crabapples; these will probably be growing in the same area, and ready at the same time, so picking should be easy. Wash the haws and chop the crabs. Put them in a preserving pan with enough water to cover them, and simmer till they are soft. You may need to add more water as the process will probably take about an hour. When soft, pour into a jelly bag and allow to strain overnight. Next day measure the juice and return to the pan with 1 lb. of sugar per pint of juice. Add the lemon juice and boil until the jelly will set when tested. Skim, pot and cover.

This produces a beautiful dark red jelly, which goes well with all kinds of cold meat.

Crabapple Jelly

It is surprising that people nowadays don't make more use of crabapples. They are still common along roadsides and on heathland, but more often than not the fruit ripens and drops from the trees unnoticed; today's children seem to get more pleasure from playing football with the apples than from picking.

We have rescued many threatened crabs. At first glance the trees seem barren; only by peering on the ground beneath them will you find the best part of the crop. When Rose and I go looking for them we forage among the autumn leaves like hungry rodents excavating the half-buried fruit, and we walk along the side of the road, heads bowed, hoping for crabs safely hidden in the grass verge.

Crabapples can be picked from August onwards and have such a superb flavour when made into jelly that they don't need any extra flavouring. Spices cannot improve their delicious scent and slightly sharp taste. Gather a good quantity of fruit, and first give them a wash, especially if you have retrieved them from the side of the road. Then chop them roughly and put in a saucepan with enough water to cover. Cook them gently until they are soft, stirring occasionally. Make sure that there is sufficient water in the saucepan, as they have a tendency to burn if they dry out. (Anyone who has had the job of cleaning a saucepan black with charred apple will appreciate this warning!) When the fruit is soft, put it through a jelly bag to strain overnight. All jelly mixtures containing apple take a long time to strain, so you must be patient. Next day measure the juice and for each pint add 1 lb. sugar. Put both in a preserving pan, and boil until a good set is achieved. Then pot and cover. You may find that the jelly has an unexpected colour; don't be put off by this – there are so many factors affecting the eventual colour of the jelly, such as the ripeness of the fruit and its genetic make-up, that any colour from bright red to yellow may result.

Having made the jelly, don't throw away the apple pulp left in the jelly bag, but use it to make crabapple cheese. (It's hard to imagine that these two products are made from the same fruit – the jelly clear and bright orange, and the cheese an odd greenish-yellow.)

Eat crabapple jelly with pork or ham.

An equally good jelly can be made from Siberian crabapples. These are grown for decoration in many gardens, but their small bright red fruit should not be allowed to go to waste. There is also a variety called 'Golden Hornet' with golden fruit that can be used as well.

Rosehip Jelly

Apart from the famous syrup this is the best way to use rosehips. Jam is too laborious a process, each hip has to be opened and the 'whiskers' (seeds) removed. So a technique such as jellying is ideal, as the pulp is discarded.

1 lb. rosehips; 2 lb. crabapples; 1 pint water; sugar; juice of 1 lemon.

Crabapples and rosehips are ripe in the early autumn, and can usually be picked from the same hedgerows. Chop the crabs and put into a saucepan with about ½ pint water and simmer till soft. Then strain through a jelly bag. Simmer the hips in the rest of the water and strain them as well. Combine the two extracts, measure and put in a preserving pan with 1 lb. sugar per pint of extract, and the lemon juice. Stir until the sugar is dissolved, and boil fast to set. Then pot and cover.

Japonica Jelly

We have a friend whose garden contains a huge japonica bush. It stands outside his door, on a bank laced with periwinkles, and each year it produces a vast quantity of fruit. As we had no japonica of our own, we asked whether we might have some fruit, and collected a bag full one sunny Saturday afternoon in October, by which time the japonicas were ripe, and sweet smelling. We didn't make the jelly straight away, but stored the fruit for a couple of weeks so that they were almost over-ripe, and had an even stronger scent.

2 lb. japonicas; juice of 1 lemon; water; sugar.

Wash the japonicas and halve them, and cook in a saucepan with enough

water to cover them. As the ripe fruit is soft, the cooking does not take
very long, but you must be careful to ensure that there is enough water
to prevent the fruit from charring at the bottom of the pan. When they
are well cooked put them through a jelly bag to strain overnight. Next
day measure the volume of juice, and for each pint add 1 lb. of sugar

and the lemon juice, and heat in a preserving pan. Boil until set. When the jelly has reached setting point, skim, pot and cover.

This makes a very good jelly indeed. It's clear, slightly sharp, and in many ways rather reminiscent of rowan jelly, although darker in colour. As we had used up a quantity of my friend's fruit, we presented him with a jar of the jelly in return. He maintained that it was a marvellous accompaniment to cheese – its fresh tang perfectly offsetting the flavour of cheddar. With Stilton or Camembert it is equally outstanding.

The japonica is a closely related species to the quince (*Cydonia vulgaris*). It has a similar appearance, scent and flavour, but can be distinguished from the quince by its long, *serrated* leaves. The commonest variety of japonica is *Cydonia japonica* which has round, yellow-skinned fruit.

Strawberry Jelly

Eliza Acton describes this as 'a very superior preserve'. Her recipe, apart from producing a magnificent jelly, is a superbly precise set of observations. It's a marvellous example of principles turned into practice.

The original directions for this delicious jelly, published in the earlier editions of this work, were the result of perfectly successful trials made in the summer of their insertion; but after much additional experience we find that the receipt may be better adapted to our varying seasons, which so much affect the quality of our fruit, and rendered more certain in its results by some alterations; we, therefore, give it anew, recommending it strongly for trial, especially to such of our readers as can command from their own gardens, ample supplies of strawberries in their best and freshest state. Like all fruit intended for preserving, they should be gathered in dry weather, after the morning dew has passed off them and be used the same day. Strip away the stalks, and put the strawberries into an enamelled stewpan if at hand, and place it very high over a clear fire so that the juice may be drawn from them gently; turn them over with a silver or a wooden spoon from time to time, and when the juice has flowed from them abundantly, let them simmer until they shrink, but be sure to take them from the fire before the juice becomes thick or pulpy from overboiling. Thirty minutes, or sometimes even longer, over a *very* slow fire, will not be too much to extract it from them. Turn them into a new, well-scalded, but *dry* sieve over a clean pan, and let them remain until the juice ceases to drop from them; strain it then through a muslin strainer, weigh it in a basin, of which the weight must first be taken, and boil it quickly in a clean preserving pan from fifteen to twenty minutes, and stir it often during the time; then take it from the fire and throw in by degrees, for every pound of juice, fourteen ounces of the best sugar coarsely pounded, stirring each portion until it is dissolved. Place the pan again over the fire, and boil the jelly – still quickly – for about a quarter of an hour. Occasionally it may need rather longer time than this, and sometimes less: the exact degree can only be ascertained by a little experience, in consequence of the juice of some varieties of the fruit being so much thinner than that of others. The preserve should jelly strongly on the skimmer, and fall in a mass from it before it is poured out; but if it is boiled beyond this point it will be spoiled. If made with richly flavoured strawberries and carefully managed, it will be a very brilliant in colour, and in flavour really equal if not superior to guava jelly; while it will retain all the delicious odour of the fruit. . . .

No skimmer or other utensil of tin should be used in making it; and an enamelled preserving pan is preferable to any other for all red fruit. It becomes very firm often after it is stored, when it appears scarcely set in the first instance; it is, however, desirable that it should jelly at once.

Modern Cookery for Private Families, Eliza Acton, 1845

Strawberry and Gooseberry Jelly

2 lb. strawberries; 2 lb. gooseberries; juice of 2 lemons; ½ pint water (approximately); sugar.

This is a marvellous jelly. It makes use of fruits which are ripe at the same time, and the presence of gooseberries gives the jelly a very good set. Use it to revive the weekend's cold roast chicken, which often tends to be rather dry on its own.

Simmer the gooseberries with the water until they are soft, and then add the strawberries. Cook the fruit until it is very soft, stirring well, and mushing with a wooden spoon to extract the juice. Then strain through a jelly bag. Measure out the juice and for each pint add 1 lb. of sugar and the lemon juice. Put these in a preserving pan and heat until the sugar is dissolved; then boil to set, remove any scum and pour into jars.

Rhubarb and Mint Jelly

Choose sticks of young pink rhubarb, clean and cut into pieces, then stew them slowly in a little water until they are soft and pulpy. Break up the rhubarb with a wooden spoon as it cooks. Strain the pulp through a jelly bag and to each pint of juice add 1 lb. sugar. Put the juice and sugar into a preserving pan and stir over a low heat until the sugar is dissolved. Then put in some leaves of fresh mint and boil until a good set is achieved. (It is easiest to put the mint in as a bundle of sprigs tied together, so that this can be removed when the jelly is ready for potting.) Pour the jelly into clean warm jars, and cover in the usual way.

You can vary this recipe by using lemon balm instead of mint. This gives the jelly a slightly sharp flavour. It goes very well with cold roast lamb, when the meat is young and sweet tasting.

Raspberry Jelly

Wring out a strong linen bag in boiling water and fill with bruised berries. Hang it in a hot oven or before the fire till the juice runs, and then press (in the cider press). To each 4 lbs juice add 5 lbs of hot crushed sugar and boil 5 minutes (it should set when cold). Pour into straight gallipots, so that the red jelly may be turned out and cut into thin slices, with which to garnish your white creams at Christmas time.

> Recipe dating from 1600 reprinted in
> *Food in England*, Dorothy Hartley,
> MacDonald, 1954

This was like a cheese both in the way it was prepared and also in the way it was used sliced and decorated. The jelly was served with different creams which were stuck with almonds, 'piony kernels', or candied angelica. These dishes were 'pretty' in the most fanciful sense of the word, and they belonged to traditions of food and eating that may seem too refined and self-indulgent for our tastes.

Barberry Jelly

1 lb. barberries; $\frac{1}{4}$ pint water; juice of 1 lemon; sugar.

The barberry (*Berberis vulgaris*) is becoming less and less common in the British Isles, although its clusters of bright red oval berries still survive in certain areas. The berries are very acid, and contain pectin, hence they jelly quite easily. In fact they can be used as a substitute for tamarinds in oriental cooking, since they have a comparable acidity.

Barberries should be picked when they are very ripe in the autumn, otherwise the jelly may be too sharp and extra sugar will need to be added to make it palatable. Wash the berries and put them in a fireproof dish. Leave this in a warm oven until the juice is running. Remove from the oven, add the water and strain through a jelly bag. Measure the volume of juice and for each pint use 1 lb. of sugar. Put both in a preserving pan, and when the sugar has dissolved add the lemon juice, bring to the boil and continue boiling until a good set is reached. Pot and cover in the usual way.

Barberry jelly was served with roast mutton or venison, and often melted and poured on top of little mutton pies.

Apple Jelly
This is not only a tasty jelly in its own right, but is a good base for herb jellies, and it is a handy way of using up windfall apples. It is best to use cookers, or the sharper varieties of eating apple for jelly.

2 lb. apples; 1 pint water; sugar.

Chop the fruit roughly – there is no need to peel or core it. Put it into a saucepan with the water and simmer until soft; stir and press the fruit with a wooden spoon while it is cooking. Then put the pulp through a jelly bag and let it strain until no more juice drips. Measure the volume of juice and for each pint take 1 lb. sugar. Return the juice to the preserving pan and stir in the sugar. Then boil rapidly to set; pot and cover.

Lemon Jelly
This is a useful jelly to make, not only because of its sharp, fresh taste, but because it's also a good starting point for many herb jellies.

lemons; sugar; water.

First wash the lemons and chop them into pieces, removing the pips Put them in a large bowl and cover with water. Let them stand overnight. Next day put them in a preserving pan, boil for 2 hours, and strain through a jelly bag. Measure the volume of juice, and for each pint add

1 lb. of sugar. Heat both in a pan until the sugar has dissolved, stirring well. Then boil until setting point is reached. Remove any scum, pour into jars and cover.

Herb Jellies

The best way to make herb jellies is to use a base such as apple or lemon and flavour it with the herb. There are methods of making these jellies by preparing an infusion of the herb, and using gelatin and artificial colouring to obtain the right appearance; mint jelly is often made this way.

If you have a good supply of fresh herbs, then make a quantity of apple or lemon jelly, divide it up into portions, and flavour each with a different herb. But it is worth experimenting with different combinations of herbs and jellies.

(1) *Basil Jelly*
1 pint apple jelly; 2 tbs. lemon juice; 6 sprigs of fresh basil.

Prepare apple jelly in the usual way (see recipe above). When you put the strained apple juice in the pan with the sugar, add the lemon juice and the basil. Boil to set, and remove the herb before pouring into jars. This is a very interesting jelly. It is sweet, and bright red but tinged with a subtle aromatic flavour. We have found that it goes surprisingly well with pheasant.

A similar jelly can be made with mint although you only need about half a dozen fresh mint leaves. You can decorate this jelly by putting a sprig of fresh flowering mint into the jar.

(2) *Marjoram Jelly*
1 pint lemon jelly; 6 sprigs marjoram.

Put the strained lemon jelly (see recipe above) into a pan with the marjoram and sugar. Boil to set, strain and pot.

The same recipe can be used to make jellies with sage or rosemary.

149

BUTTERS AND CHEESES

These preserves are best made in conjunction with jellies. When fruit is cooked and strained through a jelly bag, the juice is used for jelly, and the pulp (after sieving) for butters or cheeses. This is a very economical arrangement, far better than making these preserves only when there is a glut of fruit.

Butters: these have a soft butter-like consistency. They are made by the addition of $\frac{1}{2}$–$\frac{3}{4}$ lb. sugar to every pound of pulp. They do not keep well over long periods, so they should be made in small batches and sealed well. They are often spiced and used like jam.

Cheeses: these are much thicker preserves which are made by adding 1 lb. of sugar to every pound of pulp. They should be cooked till they are very stiff and potted in jars so that they can be turned out whole. They are usually sliced and eaten with meat, poultry and game. They should be kept for as long as possible (several months at least) before opening.

1. Butters and cheeses are best made with fruit that makes a good jelly and has no troublesome stones or pips. Thus a wide range can be used, including damsons, blackberries, apples or crabapples, quinces, gooseberries. The fruit should be washed and chopped up if necessary, put in a preserving pan with sufficient water and cooked slowly until quite soft.

2. The whole is then strained through a jelly bag; the juice used to make jelly and the pulp sieved. It is important to continue sieving until all the fruit has passed through the sieve, and only a debris of pips, stones and skins is left.

3. Weigh the pulp and depending on whether you wish to make a butter or a cheese, weigh out the appropriate quantity of sugar. Put both in a preserving pan, stir until the sugar is dissolved and continue boiling until the required consistency is reached.

If you are making a cheese and the fruit pulp is rather thin and fluid, it is as well to reduce this before adding the sugar. Cheeses should be cooked until they are so thick that a spoon drawn across the bottom of the pan leaves a clean line.

Butters should be potted when they reach a thick creamy consistency.
4. Potting.

Butters: these should be put into small jars or pots as for jam. The jars should be warmed. If you intend to use the preserve quickly then jam pot covers can be used. If you want to keep the butter for some time, then it is best to sterilize the jars in hot water and to reinforce the cover with parchment paper.

Cheeses: use straight-sided jars for cheeses so that they can be turned out whole when required. Before potting brush the inside of the warmed jars with a little olive oil or glycerine to make turning out easier. Pour in the cheese hot and cover with a waxed circle and plastic like a jam. The longer the cheese can be kept before opening the better, but once it has been turned out, it should be used up as quickly as possible.

5. Like other preserves, butters and cheeses should be stored in a dry, dark cupboard.

Butters will keep for 3–6 months without spoiling, but as they have a lower sugar content than cheeses, they should be used up fairly quickly.

Cheeses on the other hand benefit from long keeping and are at their best after 6 months' storage. You may be able to keep them for more than a year.

Plum Butter

Choose ripe, dark-skinned plums for this butter. Slit the skins and put the fruit to cook in a pan with a little water. When they are soft press through a sieve until only the skins and stones are left. Then for each lb. of pulp add ¾ lb. sugar, put these together in a preserving pan and bring to the boil, stirring occasionally. Then continue to cook until the right consistency is reached. Pot and cover in the usual way.

In fact this butter keeps rather well – we have eaten samples that were well over a year old and deliciously smooth.

Plum butter is a useful standby for making plum sauce in Chinese cookery, especially for that marvellous ceremonial dish, Peking duck.

A similar butter can be made using damsons in place of plums.

Apple Butter

This preserve is quite special to a small section of the American population – the Pennsylvania Dutch. It is a thanksgiving dish, and commemorates their voyage to America in 1734.

1 quart sweet cider; 4 lb. ripe apples; 1 lb. brown sugar; 1 tsp. ground cloves; 2 tsp. ground cinnamon; ½ tsp. ground allspice.

Put the cider into a pan and boil it until it is reduced by half. Then peel, core and chop the apples and add to the cider. Cook slowly until the fruit is tender; you will need to stir the mixture frequently. Then work the apple mixture through a sieve and return the puree to the pan with the sugar and spices. Simmer until the mixture thickens, stirring well. Pour the butter into jars and cover in the usual way.

Apple butter is very like a nineteenth-century apple 'marmalade' made in England; in both cases the apples were cooked in cider, pulped and mixed with sugar. This 'marmalade' was said to be 'very nice, and extremely wholesome as supper for the juveniles, and for the aged, eaten with cream or milk'.

Damson Cheese

This is a very old country dish. Since a large quantity of fruit is needed to produce a relatively small amount of the cheese, it was common at a time when damsons were also common, and picked by the basketful off heavily laden trees. It's an elegant, luxurious dish, and was a regular feature of huge Victorian dinner parties. Cheeses were served as desserts in the grand style. They were tall constructions, often more than a foot high, fashioned by piling cheeses on top of each other. The damson cheeses were set at one end of the table with elaborate crabapple cheeses at the other – a startling contrast in colour.

Put the damsons into an earthenware casserole dish with the lid on, and cook slowly in the oven at 250°F until the juice runs and the flesh is soft. (Originally the damsons were put into the bread oven when it was cooling down after the loaves had been 'drawn' – a sensible way of conserving fuel.) Rub the damsons through a sieve, until only the stones and skins are left. Crack the stones, remove the kernels, chop and add to the pulp. This gives a characteristic almond flavour to the cheese. Then put the pulp in a preserving pan with an equal weight of sugar, which has been previously warmed in the oven. Boil well till the cheese is very thick and put it into wide-mouthed, straight-sided glass jars, the insides of which have been moistened with a little olive oil. Cover and do not use for at least 6 months.

In fact cheeses keep well and those at least 2 years old are said to be excellent. By this time the top has begun to crust with sugar, and it has shrunk a little from the sides of the jar. This is useful, since the cheese should be turned out whole onto a plate when required. A knife inserted round the sides of the jar helps to ease the cheese out.

Damson cheese can either be served whole as a dessert with port wine poured over it, or cut into thick slices and eaten with cold pheasant or other game.

Crabapple Cheese

Like damson cheese, crabapple or apple cheese was a feature of Victorian dinner tables. It was eaten at Christmas as a dessert, studded with hazelnuts and decorated with whirls of whipped cream; a sensible counterbalance to the dark effect of damson cheese and port wine.

It is best to make crabapple cheese at the same time as the jelly. Chop the crabapples so that you cut across the core to expose the kernel – this is important to the flavour of the cheese. After cooking and straining through a jelly bag, sieve the pulp until only skins and pips are left. For each pound of pulp add 1 lb. of sugar; put these into a pan and bring slowly to the boil. Cook until the cheese is thick, then pot and cover.

Keep crabapple cheese for several months before using, then turn it out whole, slice and serve it with cold meat.

Blackberry Cheese

When you make bramble jelly, keep the pulp after straining the fruit for use in blackberry cheese. Press through a sieve until only pips are left. Then measure out 1 lb. of sugar for each pound of pulp; put into a preserving pan with the juice of 1 lemon. Bring to the boil slowly, stirring well, and then continue to cook until the cheese has thickened. Pot and cover.

When turned out whole and cut into thick slices this is a very effective preserve. Chunks of it go well with cold pheasant, eaten like a kind of 'fruit paté' on brown bread.

Cranberry Cheese

The cranberry (*Vaccinium oxycoccus*) was an English fruit taken to America by the first settlers. It flourished in the Fens before these were drained, but now it is a rare sight and grows only in the north of England, Scotland and Wales. When the cranberry was introduced into America, it was absorbed into American cookery and found its way into a number of famous recipes.

1 lb. cranberries; ½ pint water; 2 oz. seedless raisins; 2 oz. chopped walnuts; sugar.

Simmer the cranberries in the water until they are soft, then strain through a jelly bag. Take the pulp and press it through a sieve. Then for each pound of pulp weigh out 1 lb. sugar. Put the pulp and the sugar into a preserving pan with the raisins and walnuts and bring slowly to the boil, stirring well. Continue to cook until the cheese is the right consistency – this will probably take about 20 minutes. Then transfer the cheese to a suitable jar, cover and store.

When this cheese is used, it should be turned out whole and decorated with thinly sliced oranges.

Chapter 9

MARMALADES

To begin with, the word marmalade did not refer to citrus fruits at all. In the middle ages 'marmelade' (or 'cotignac' in France) was made from quinces, honey and wine, and was flavoured with ginger, cinnamon and galingale. A similar type of preserve had been made by the Romans, who called it 'melimelum'; this was transformed into the Portuguese word for quince – 'marmelo' and then to 'marmelade'. This word was used to describe a whole range of jam-like products right up to the nineteenth century, and the terminology became even more confusing when the now familiar citrus marmalade was developed in the eighteenth century. Fortunately the word is now confined to this type of preserve and has lost its broader usage.

Marmalade as we know it required oranges in cheap and plentiful supply. Bitter oranges had been brought to Britain in the fourteenth century in Spanish ships, but although they occasionally appeared in the lists of wealthy households, they were a very expensive luxury. However they gradually became a more familiar sight in London markets and kitchens during the Elizabethan age when they were often called 'portyngales' – a reference to the fact that they came from Portugal.

One feature of the big country estates that blossomed in the English countrysides in the seventeenth century was the orangery. This was a fashionable imitation of the habits of the French aristocracy. Glasshouses were also quite common, and were used for growing vines and nectarines as well as orange and lemon trees.

At the same time the first recipes for a type of orange marmalade began to appear. By this time the heavy spicing of the medieval 'marmelade' had been dropped, but the resulting preserve was, like its predecessor, solid and intended to be cut in pieces rather than spread. The pieces were printed with moulds, sprinkled with sugar and eaten as sweetmeats.

Take Orenges and pare off as thinne as is possible the uppermost rind of the Orenge, yet as by no means to alter the colour of the Orenge, then steepe in fair water changing the water twice a day till you finde no bitterness of taste therein then ... boile them in Rosewater till they breake and to every 1 lb of pulpe put 1 lb of sugar, and so mashe and stirre and rub thro' a sieve into boxes, and so use as you shall see occasion.

But it is generally agreed that orange marmalade, as we know it, was first made by the Scottish Keiller family early in the eighteenth century:

One morning a ship from Spain, long buffeted by easterly gales, reached Tayside and deposited a cargo of oranges. Among those who gathered at the quayside was James Keiller. The oranges were going cheap, and James was tempted to buy a considerable quantity – rashly, as it seemed, for owing to their bitter taste he was unable to sell them. What was to be done? His thrifty and resourceful young wife supplied the answer. We may assume that she was already skilled in the making of jams and jellies; but little could she have dreamed, as she stood over her kitchen fire, boiling and testing, that the result of her experiment would achieve world-wide renown.

The Scots Kitchen, F. Marian McNeill, Blackie, 1929

The important difference between this and earlier marmalades was that Keiller included thin strips of orange peel in the preserve.

For quite some time marmalade remained a Scottish speciality and was regarded with suspicion in England, although it was enjoyed by people who had visited Scotland or had friends who made marmalade themselves. Thus Boswell on returning from his visit to Scotland in 1771 wrote to Dr Johnson: 'My wife is sending you some marmalade of her own making.'

However, marmalade was not properly introduced into England until 1870, when Mrs Cooper, a grocer's wife from Oxford, was given a recipe and decided to make the preserve on a small scale. By this time bitter and sweet oranges were cheap and plentiful and lemons and limes were imported in large quantities from the West Indies. Mrs Cooper's marmalade was very popular and quickly became the standard breakfast food of undergraduates, to such an extent that Cooper, like Keiller, had to set up a factory to cope with the demand.

The latter part of the nineteenth century saw a gradual decline in the size of the breakfast. In large households, the rich had been used to pies, devilled mutton chops, curried eggs, kippered salmon and even more outrageous dishes such as stuffed pig's ears. But with the growth of cities and the changes in working habits, the large, time-consuming breakfast went out of fashion. It was replaced by a simple, less weighty meal that suited the businessman much better. Before taking a coach to the city, he would have boiled eggs, or fried egg and bacon, followed by toast with preserves and a cup of tea or coffee. The appearance of marmalade at this time meant that it was quickly taken up, particularly in middle-class families.

From the turn of the century, marmalade was a standard item on the breakfast table, either in its original unassuming stoneware jars, or in many-sided pots made of fragile china and decorated with floral designs. It was dug out with an ornate spoon, and spread onto hot buttered toast. While the preserve is best known as a breakfast food, it does have many other uses, especially in traditional Scottish cookery. As well as spreading marmalade on oatcakes or wholemeal scones, the Scots eat it with pork, boiled ham, duck or goose, either like a chutney or in the form of marmalade sauce, using a recipe that includes port wine and mushroom ketchup. They also make marmalade cake and marmalade pudding.

Much of what we have said about jam making applies equally to marmalades. There are, however, several other important points to remember:

1. The best marmalade is made from bitter Seville oranges. In fact only about a quarter of the oranges imported into this country come from Seville; the rest come from Malaga and Sicily. Shipments begin to arrive in December and continue for about three months, so the best time to make marmalade is at the end of January, when the fruit is plentiful and cheap, and before the slightly poorer end of season fruit arrives.

Other citrus fruit such as lemons and grapefruit can be used for marmalade at almost any time of the year. If you try to bulk out supplies with sweet oranges as well as Sevilles, you may find that the marmalade has a cloudy appearance. Tangerines are not suitable for marmalade unless mixed with some other citrus fruit.

2. The fruit should be washed well before using. If the skins are very dirty they can be scrubbed. Soak the fruit for a couple of minutes in boiling water, and the skins will peel quite easily.

3. The pectin in citrus fruits is mainly found in the pips and white pith, and this needs to be brought into solution. The actual methods of preparing the fruit vary depending on the type of marmalade required and the fruits themselves. For example, chunky Seville marmalade contains slices cut from whole peel with pith, whilst jelly marmalade is simply thin slices of peel in jelly. The pith and pips are usually put into a muslin bag and removed at the end of the cooking time before the sugar is added. (Chunky Seville marmalade is one exception.)

Chop the peel by hand or by using a marmalade cutter. The thicker the slices the longer they take to soften. But don't be tempted to use a coarse mincer for this operation as it produces a paste-like marmalade.

The precise methods of peeling and preparing the fruit are given in the various recipes.

4. Keep the cut peel in a little water otherwise it will dry out. There is no virtue in leaving the peel to soak overnight, unless you are unable to make the marmalade in one session.

5. The fruit is cooked with water to soften the peel and also to extract the pectin. The proportions of fruit to water vary depending on the recipe and quantity of marmalade being made. Generally, 2 pints of water are allowed per pound of fruit in an open pan, and one pint per pound in a closed pressure cooker. For very large quantities the amount of water can be reduced.

Normally the pulp and peel are cooked with the pith and pips which are tied in a muslin bag. Cooking usually takes 2–3 hours, or until the peel has softened, so that it disintegrates when squeezed between the fingers; only then can the sugar be added.

6. Add the sugar when the peel is soft and the excess water has been boiled off. If you add the sugar too soon, the peel tends to toughen. But the peel should not be over-cooked as this will spoil the colour of the marmalade.

After the sugar has dissolved, the marmalade should be boiled rapidly until setting point is reached. This usually takes 15–20 minutes. While citrus fruits have a good setting quality, the setting point is quickly passed, so test carefully and don't boil for too long.

7. When setting point has been reached, skim the marmalade to prevent scum adhering to the pieces of peel. Allow the marmalade to cool a little before pouring it into the jars; this prevents the peel rising after potting. Stir gently, then transfer the marmalade to warm jars, and cover like jam (see p. 123).

Seville Orange Marmalade
3 lb. Seville oranges; juice of 2 lemons; 6 pints water; 6 lb. sugar.

The skins of the fruit are often quite dirty so wash them well. Then cut them in half and squeeze out the juice and remove the pips. Cut the peel into shreds and put it into a pan with the pips (tied in a muslin bag), the water, lemon juice, and orange pulp. Simmer for about $1\frac{1}{2}$ hours until the peel is very soft. Then remove the muslin bag, and squeeze it well. Stir in the sugar until it has completely dissolved and boil rapidly until setting point is reached. Let the marmalade stand for about 10 minutes then give it a final stir before transferring it to jars and covering.

You can spice the marmalade, for example by adding 2 tsp. coriander seeds to each lb. of fruit. These should be put into the muslin bag with the pips.

Spirits such as whisky and brandy can also be used to flavour the marmalade.

There are several types of ready prepared orange pulp in cans for making into marmalade. In these the oranges are chopped and ready for mixing with sugar and water; so the process takes no more than $\frac{1}{2}$ hour. However the quality of the marmalade is not very good; it is insipid and the peel is often chopped so finely as to be almost unnoticeable in the finished product. Having tried some of these, we can only say that there is really no substitute for fresh fruit, roughly chopped and properly prepared.

Dark Coarse-Cut Marmalade
3 lb. Seville oranges; 1 lemon; 7 pints water; 6 lb. sugar; 2 tbs. black treacle.

Wash the fruit, cut in half and squeeze out the juice and pips. Cut the peel into thick shreds and chop the flesh roughly. Put the flesh, juice, peel and pips (tied in a muslin bag) into the water and boil gently for about 2 hours until the peel has softened and the volume has been reduced by half. Then remove the bag of pips and stir in the sugar and treacle. When the sugar has dissolved boil rapidly until setting point is reached. You may like to add some whisky at this stage (about 2 tsp. per lb. of fruit); it makes the marmalade deliciously rich and potent. After stirring in the liquor, allow the marmalade to cool a little before potting and covering.

This marmalade needs to be stored for several months at least before opening. We have eaten it aged and syrupy, more than 2 years old.

Jelly Marmalade
4 lb. Seville oranges; 1 lb. lemons; 5 pints water; sugar.

First peel off the outer rind of the fruit very thinly and cut it into strips. Put it into about 1 pint of water and cook until quite tender. Then drain, keeping the rind and the liquid.

Meanwhile chop the flesh of the oranges and lemons after taking off any pith, and put into another pan with the rest of the water. Simmer gently until the fruit is very soft. Then add the liquid in which the rind was boiled and continue to cook for a few minutes more. Strain through a jelly bag. Do not squeeze the bag or the marmalade will be cloudy.

Then measure the volume of juice and for each pint add 1 lb. of sugar. Put both in the pan with the strips of rind. Stir until the sugar has dissolved then boil rapidly to setting point. This will probably take 10–15 minutes. Allow the marmalade to cool a little, give it a final stir to disperse the shreds, then pot and cover.

Apricot and Orange Marmalade

This is an example of the way additional fruits can be used to vary the conventional marmalade.

2 lb. Seville oranges; 2 lemons; 12 oz. dried apricots; 8 pints water; 8 lb. sugar.

Wash the oranges and lemons and cut them into quarters; remove the pips and put them in a muslin bag. Pare off the peel and cut into strips. Then chop the flesh of the citrus fruit and the apricots and put this into a preserving pan with the water, peel and muslin bag. Leave overnight.

Next day bring the mixture to the boil and simmer for about 2 hours or until the peel is very tender and disintegrates when squeezed. After this add the sugar, bring the mixture to the boil and cook rapidly for about 20 minutes or until setting point is reached. Then remove from the heat, and allow the marmalade to cool a little. Pot and cover.

This marmalade has a thick, pulpy consistency rather like a jam.

Orange Marmalade Made with Honey

It was quite common practice in the nineteenth century to use honey rather than sugar in marmalades. This is a recipe from Mrs Beeton:

To 1 quart of the juice and pulp of Seville oranges allow 2 lbs honey, 1 lb of the rind.

Peel the oranges and boil the rind in water until tender, and cut into strips. Take away the pips from the juice and pulp, and put it with the honey and chips into a preserving pan; boil all together for about ½ hr, or until the marmalade is of the proper consistency; put it into pots; and when cold cover down with bladders.

The Book of Household Management, Mrs Beeton, 1861

Three Fruit Marmalade

This is a very useful standby recipe when quantities of marmalade are needed at short notice; it does not require seasonal Seville oranges.

3 lb. fruit (made up of 2 sweet oranges, 4 lemons, 2 grapefruit); 6 pints water; 6 lb. sugar.

First wash the oranges and lemons, halve them and squeeze out the juice and pips. Also wash and peel the grapefruit, making sure you remove the pith and stringy parts of the fruit. Then chop up the flesh of all the fruit and cut the peel into thin strips. Put the peel, flesh and juice into a pan with the water, and add the pips and pith tied in a muslin bag. Cook gently for about 1½ hours or until the peel is very soft. Don't be tempted to rush this process, or the peel will not be sufficiently cooked and your marmalade may not set as a result.

When the peel is soft remove the muslin bag and squeeze it well. Add the sugar and stir until it is dissolved; boil rapidly until setting point is reached. Let the marmalade cool a little; then pot and cover in the usual way.

Lime Marmalade

If you manage to find a supply of cheap limes then it is well worth making some of this marmalade; it has a delicious, refreshing flavour – perfect as an early morning reviver.

1½ lb. limes; 3 pints water; 3 lb. sugar.

First clean the limes and remove the stalk end of each fruit. Then put them in the water to simmer for about 2 hours until the fruit is very soft. Remove and slice the limes very thinly into small pieces, discarding the pips. Add the fruit and any excess juice that has collected during slicing to the original water in the pan. Then add the sugar and stir until it has dissolved. After this boil rapidly until setting point is reached; allow the marmalade to cool a little before potting and covering.

Lemon and Grapefruit Marmalade

When we need marmalade and there are no Seville oranges, we often use this recipe.

2 lb. grapefruit; 1 lb. lemons; 6 pints water; 6 lb. sugar.

Wash the fruit and pare off the outer rind. Cut into thin strips. Then remove the pith and pips and put these into a muslin bag. Chop the flesh roughly making sure no juice is lost. Put all these ingredients into a pan with the water and simmer for about $1\frac{1}{2}$ hours or until the peel is very soft and disintegrates when squeezed. Remove the muslin bag, squeeze it well and then add the sugar. Stir until dissolved and then boil rapidly until setting point is reached. Allow the marmalade to cool a little before potting and covering in the usual way.

Ginger Marmalade

One of my real favourites. I remember schoolboy breakfasts that began with Finnan haddock steamed in milk and finished with slices of toast and ginger marmalade spread as thickly as possible. There are really two types: one is made from apples and ginger – this isn't a marmalade at all but a kind of exotic jam; the other is a blend of oranges, lemons and ginger, a true marmalade.

2 lb. Seville oranges; 2 lemons; 1 oz. root ginger; 7 pints water; 8 oz. preserved ginger; 6 lb. sugar.

First wash and halve the oranges and lemons; then squeeze out the juice and pips. Strain the juice into a bowl and tie the pips and the root ginger in a muslin bag. Cut the orange and lemon peel into strips and put into a pan with the water, juice and muslin bag. Simmer until the peel is quite soft and disintegrates when squeezed between the finger and thumb. This will probably take about 2 hours. Then remove the muslin bag, add the preserved ginger, chopped finely, and stir in the sugar. When it has dissolved, boil rapidly until setting point is reached. Allow the marmalade to cool a little, stir well to disperse the ginger; pot and cover in the usual way.

Chapter 10

SOME ODDITIES:
CANDIED FRUIT AND FLOWERS,
HONEYS AND CURDS

CANDIED FRUIT AND FLOWERS

The principle of candying involves covering the fruit with a dilute
hot syrup which is gradually concentrated day by day so that the fruit
is impregnated with sugar. It is important to do this slowly in stages
to give the sugar time to penetrate as water in the fruit diffuses out.
If candying is hurried the fruit will become tough and wrinkled.
Personally it is not a technique for which we can find much enthusiasm,
except where the product is exceptional and useful, as is the case with
candied peel.

Candied Peel

This was a popular sweetmeat in France as early as the fourteenth century, when oranges were one of the luxuries of the rich. The peel was first boiled in water and then allowed to steep in honey; it was then drained and packed in layers sprinkled with powdered ginger.

Nowadays the process is slightly different. Take the peel from oranges, lemons and grapefruit, wash and cut into pieces. Then boil for about 1 hour in water. Drain and make up a syrup of 1 lb. sugar to 1 pint water. (Ideally ½ lb. of sugar and ½ lb. glucose should be used, as this gives the peel a good appearance and helps it keep well.) Bring the syrup to the boil and pour it over the peel. Leave for several days. Then strain off the syrup, boil it up again and pour over the fruit. Repeat this operation every day until the peel looks clear and the syrup is very thick. Remove the peel and dry it on trays in a very slow oven (100°F). Store in bottles or boxes between layers of greaseproof paper.

Candied Barberries

When the barberry was more common, bunches were dipped into sugar that had been boiled to a syrup, and left there for several hours. The berries were then removed and the sugar was boiled further to candy point; the berries were put back into this and left until candied. When ready they were left to dry off, and put into jars.

Candied Cowslips

At the beginning of the eighteenth century, home confectionery was flourishing. Housewives produced all manner of cakes, biscuits and wafers, and also sweetmeats such as almond comfits, caramel oranges, ginger tablets, apricot chips and chocolate, which in those days included a large number of unlikely ingredients: ground almonds and pistachio nuts, aniseed, cinnamon and musk. These sweet-making cooks were also familiar with the art of candying flowers. These were eaten as sweets, used for decorating cakes and puddings and were also thought to have valuable medicinal properties; candied scabious flowers for example were used 'to clean the heart and lungs'. In fact a great variety of flowers was used: daisies, forget-me-nots, narcissi, apple and almond blossom, but perhaps the most well known is the candied cowslip.

There were two different ways of candying these flowers. The first

166

involved the use of gum arabic, which was steeped in water for 3 days until it dissolved. Often orange flower water was used for this part of the process. The cowslips were coated with a thin film of gum using a paint brush. They were then dipped in fine sifted sugar and allowed to dry by being strung across a chimney.

The second method was much closer to the conventional methods of preserving with sugar. The flowers were collected on a dry day, only the yellow blossoms being used for candying. Sugar was heated in a pan with the minimum possible quantity of water. The pan was taken off the heat, the flowers were added a few at a time, and the whole was stirred until the candied flowers were dry enough to put into glasses or jars.

For those who have an inclination towards such delicate 'sweet nothings', candied flowers are quite simple to make. But we should discourage the picking of cowslips for that purpose nowadays. They are no longer common and certainly picking in the quantities suggested by old recipes would be quite thoughtless. Choose flowers that are common and widespread in their distribution and if you do pick them don't completely strip one patch but select a few flowers from various sites.

Candied Tomatoes
4 lb. yellow tomatoes; 2 lemons; 1 lb. sugar; 1 pint water.

First peel the tomatoes after putting them into boiling water for a couple of minutes. Then make up a syrup by boiling the sugar and the water; add the sliced lemons and remove any scum that forms. Put the tomatoes carefully into the syrup and simmer slowly for 15 minutes. Then remove them and put onto a sieve to drain. Boil up the syrup once more until it is thick, add the tomatoes and simmer for 1 hour, or until they are soft but not mushy.

Take out the tomatoes, let them drain, and then flatten them with a wooden spoon. Lay them out on trays and let them dry in a very slow oven (100°F). Store the candied tomatoes in glass jars in a dark cupboard.

Candied Angelica
When I was a small boy, I was continually amazed by angelica; I simply

could not believe that those sticky, bright green strips patterned on cakes really derived from a plant. They came within the whole area of sweet things that were made from sugar, flavouring and colouring; indeed I can even remember doubting their edibility on finding pieces sticking ominously out of layers of icing and marzipan.

But, as I later discovered, angelica is quite edible, and a delicious sweet morsel. In fact it was a common home-made product up to the middle of the nineteenth century, since it was seldom sold in markets.

There are two distinct plants bearing the name angelica: one is wild angelica (*Angelica sylvestris*) which has pink flowers and purplish stems and is found growing in damp places. The other is garden angelica (*Angelica archangelica*), which has green stems and white flowers and is cultivated in many gardens. This is the plant whose stems are candied. Pick the stems in May or June when they are young and green. Cut them into short lengths (about 4 inches) and put them to boil in water for 5 minutes. Lift them out and scrape off any tough fibrous strands from the outside of the stems. Then make up a syrup of 1 lb. sugar to 1 pint water and simmer the angelica in this until tender. Remove from the heat and leave the angelica in the syrup for several days. Drain off the syrup, boil it up and pour it over the angelica. Repeat this process each day until the stems are stiff with sugar. At this stage take them out, let them drain and then put them on trays to dry in a very slow oven (100°F). When ready the angelica should be stored in bottles or in boxes in layers separated by greaseproof paper. If kept in bottles, the angelica should not be exposed to the light.

HONEYS

Parsley Honey
5 oz. parsley; 1½ pints water; 1 lb. sugar; juice of 1 lemon.

Parsley honey was made a great deal in the country during the Second World War when honey itself was scarce; it is a good way of using up parsley that has seeded. First collect the parsley and dry it well. Chop and put into a preserving pan with the water; then boil until the volume is reduced to approximately 1 pint. Stir in the sugar and add the lemon juice. Boil for about 20 minutes until the mixture has a thick honey-like consistency. Pot and cover while still hot.

Rob of Mulberries
This is reputedly an old Arabian recipe – 'rob' is the Arabic word for dense.

Take some mulberries and put them into a pan with a very small amount of water. Cook gently until the fruit is mushy. Then strain through a jelly bag, and for each pint of juice add ½ pint of liquid honey. Mix the juice and the honey well, and simmer until the mixture is reduced to a thick honey-like consistency.

The rob should be used soon after it is made as it does not keep well. It can be used like honey or as a basis for a drink. Robs can be made from other fruits like blackcurrants; in his *Diary of a Country Parson*, James Woodforde records that on 22 March 1773 he

. . . Got up this morning with a comical kind of sore throat, not much pain, had something of it Yesterday, rather worse today – made use of Port Wine Yesterday, pretty freely, and some black Currant Rob.

CURDS

These are curious preserves; in fact they are really 'semi-preserves' since they include ingredients other than the fruit and preservative (namely eggs and butter), and they have a shelf life of a few weeks at the most.

It is important to thicken a curd *very* slowly, without boiling, otherwise the combination of eggs and acid will cause curdling. If this does occur, remove the mixture from the heat and whisk very sharply. The curd can then be replaced over the heat if the curdling has disappeared.

Remember that the curd will thicken as it cools, so do not over-cook.

Lemon Curd
grated rind and juice of 4 lemons; 4 eggs; 4 oz. butter; 1 lb. sugar.

Grate the rind of the lemons very carefully so that only the yellow 'zest' is removed. Then squeeze the juice from the fruit. Put the lemon rind and juice, the sugar and the butter into the top of a double saucepan, or a basin over a saucepan of hot water. Simmer until the sugar has dissolved, stirring well. Then add the beaten eggs and continue to simmer very gently until the mixture begins to thicken and coat the back of the wooden spoon. If you have difficulty getting the curd to thicken, add a small amount of ground rice to the mixture and stir this in well. Then pour the curd into warm jars and cover in the usual way. Store in a cool place and use within a month of making. Because curds do not keep well, they should be made in small batches.

A similar curd can be made using oranges instead of lemons, or a mixture of oranges and lemons can be used.

Blackberry Curd

12 oz. blackberries; 4 oz. cooking apples; juice of 1 lemon; 4 eggs; 4 oz. butter; 1 lb. sugar.

Wash the blackberries, peel core and chop the apples and put both into a pan without water to cook very slowly, so that the fruit is softened and the juice drawn out. Then sieve the mixture well, and put the pulp into the top of a double saucepan with the lemon juice, butter and sugar. Simmer very gently until the sugar has dissolved, stirring occasionally. Then add the beaten eggs and continue to simmer until the mixture thickens. Pot and cover in the usual way; store in a cool place.

171

Marrow Curd

1 lb. cooked marrow pulp; juice of 2 lemons; 4 oz. butter; 2 eggs;
1 lb. sugar.

Peel the marrow and remove the pith; chop into small pieces and
cook very slowly without water until soft. Then press through a sieve
until a smooth pulp is obtained, and weigh the pulp – you may need to
adjust the quantities of the other ingredients appropriately. Put the
marrow, lemon juice, sugar and butter into the top of a double saucepan
and simmer gently until the sugar has dissolved, stirring occasionally.
Add the beaten eggs and continue to cook slowly until the curd begins
to thicken. Pot and cover in the usual way.

A NOTE ON BOTTLING,
CANNING AND FREEZING

These methods of preserving are really outside the scope of our book, but we have decided to mention them for the sake of completeness. There are a number of useful publications that deal with bottling, canning and freezing in detail, so we shall simply list some of the advantages and disadvantages of these techniques, and refer readers to the most helpful sources of information.

Bottling is in a sense the most traditional of these methods; it has been widely used for fruit and to a lesser extent vegetables. Bottled fruit is a useful standby during the winter but as with many other methods of preserving, the product tends to deteriorate after a few months. Bottled vegetables are not something to be recommended; the actual preparation and sterilization must be strictly controlled otherwise there is a real danger of soil bacteria such as *Salmonella* and *Clostridium* developing and these can be extremely toxic. And the notion of bottling a vegetable like asparagus strikes us as a waste of an excellent food; it should be eaten fresh during its short season, not stored, bottled up until it loses all taste and texture. There is one other disadvantage to bottling and that is the cost of the special Kilner jars; this must be considered if preservation is to be a process based on economy.

The same economic disadvantages apply to canning; you need a special piece of apparatus for sealing the open-ended cans, and then there is the cost of the cans themselves. It is doubtful whether such an expensive method can justify its use; home-canning is not likely to improve on the standards of factory-made produce. Both canning and bottling rely on heat sterilization as the means of preservation – bacteria are killed by the high temperatures, and the design of the containers prevents access of bacteria from outside.

Finally freezing. Nowadays this is a very useful and easy method of storing food, but the important point about freezing is that it should not replace other methods of preservation; it should be used with them.

The choice is not simply 'make jam' or 'put the fruit into the freezer'; both should be considered. Of course frozen food is no substitute for fresh, whether it be fruit, vegetables, meat or fish, but if you can afford to buy the freezer *and* buy food in bulk, then it is worthwhile at least in economic terms. And there are other advantages as well. First of all, the deepfreeze allows a lot of food to be stored in a relatively small space; a freezer is useful for storing prepared dishes as well as for 'raw' produce, and it can be a life-saver when there is nothing fresh in the larder.

Some useful sources of information are:

1. *Fresh from the Freezer* by Marye Cameron-Smith (Penguin)
2. *The Penguin Freezer Cookbook* by Helge Rubinstein and Sheila Bush (Penguin)
3. *The Good Housekeeping Cookery Book*
4. *The Home Preservation of Fruit and Vegetables* (H.M.S.O. Bulletin 21)

WEIGHTS, MEASURES
AND TEMPERATURES

LIQUID MEASURES

British

1 quart	= 2 pints	= 40 fl. oz.	
1 pint	= 4 gills	= 20 fl. oz.	
½ pint	= 2 gills		
	or 1 cup	= 10 fl. oz.	
¼ pint	= 8 tablespoons	= 5 fl. oz.	
	1 tablespoon	= just over ½ fl. oz.	
	1 dessertspoon =	$\frac{1}{3}$ fl. oz.	
	1 teaspoon	= $\frac{1}{6}$ fl. oz.	

Metric

1 litre = 10 decilitres (dl) = 100 centilitres (cl) = 1000 millilitres (ml)

Approximate equivalents

BRITISH	METRIC
1 quart	1.1 litre
1 pint	6 dl
½ pint	3 dl
¼ pint (1 gill)	1.5 dl
1 tablespoon	15 ml
1 dessertspoon	10 ml
1 teaspoon	5 ml

METRIC	BRITISH
1 litre	35 fl. oz.
½ litre (5 dl)	18 fl. oz.
¼ litre (2.5 dl)	9 fl. oz.
1 dl	3½ fl. oz.

American

1 quart	= 2 pints	= 32 fl. oz.
1 pint	= 2 cups	= 16 fl. oz.
	1 cup	= 8 fl. oz.
	1 tablespoon =	$\frac{1}{3}$ fl. oz.
	1 teaspoon =	$\frac{1}{6}$ fl. oz.

Approximate equivalents

BRITISH	AMERICAN
1 quart	$2\frac{1}{2}$ pints
1 pint	$1\frac{1}{4}$ pints
$\frac{1}{2}$ pint	10 fl. oz. ($1\frac{1}{4}$ cups)
$\frac{1}{4}$ pint (1 gill)	5 fl. oz.
1 tablespoon	$1\frac{1}{2}$ tablespoons
1 dessertspoon	1 tablespoon
1 teaspoon	$\frac{1}{3}$ fl. oz.

AMERICAN	BRITISH
1 quart	$1\frac{1}{2}$ pints + 3 tablespoons (32 fl. oz.)
1 pint	$\frac{3}{4}$ pint + 2 tablespoons (16 fl. oz.)
1 cup	$\frac{1}{2}$ pint − 2 tablespoons (8 fl. oz.)

SOLID MEASURES

British

16 oz. = 1 lb.

Metric

1000 grammes = 1 kilogramme

Approximate equivalents

BRITISH	METRIC
1 lb. (16 oz.)	400 g
$\frac{1}{2}$ lb. (8 oz.)	200 g
$\frac{1}{4}$ lb. (4 oz.)	100 g
1 oz.	25 g

WEIGHTS, MEASURES AND TEMPERATURES

METRIC	BRITISH
1 kilo (1000 g)	2 lb. 3 oz.
½ kilo (500 g)	1 lb. 2 oz.
¼ kilo (250 g)	9 oz.
100 g	3½ oz.

OVEN TEMPERATURES

TEMPERATURE EQUIVALENTS
FOR OVEN THERMOSTAT MARKINGS

Degrees Fahrenheit	Gas Regulo mark	Degrees Centigrade
225	$\frac{1}{4}$	110
250	$\frac{1}{2}$	130
275	1	140
300	2	150
325	3	170
350	4	180
375	5	190
400	6	200
425	7	220
450	8	230
475	9	240

INDEX